HISTORICAL RECORD OF THE FIFTH
OR
PRINCESS CHARLOTTE OF
WALES'S REGIMENT OF DRAGOON GUARDS

RICHARD CANNON

Table of Contents

PREFACE.

The character and credit of the British Army must chiefly depend upon the zeal and ardour, by which all who enter into its service are animated, and consequently it is of the highest importance that any measure calculated to excite the spirit of emulation, by which alone great and gallant actions are achieved, should be adopted.

Nothing can more fully tend to the accomplishment of this desirable object, than a full display of the noble deeds with which the Military History of our country abounds. To hold forth these bright examples to the imitation of the youthful soldier, and thus to incite him to emulate the meritorious conduct of those who have preceded him in their honourable career, are among the motives that have given rise to the present publication.

The operations of the British Troops are, indeed, announced in the 'London Gazette,' from whence they are transferred into the public prints: the achievements of our armies are thus made known at the time of their occurrence, and receive the tribute of praise and admiration to which they are entitled. On extraordinary occasions, the Houses of Parliament have been in the habit of conferring on the Commanders, and the Officers and Troops acting under their orders, expressions of approbation and of thanks for their skill and bravery, and these testimonials, confirmed by the high honour of their Sovereign's Approbation, constitute the reward which the soldier most highly prizes.

It has not, however, until late years, been the practice (which appears to have long prevailed in some of the Continental armies) for British Regiments to keep regular records of their services and achievements. Hence some difficulty has been experienced in obtaining, particularly from the old Regiments, an authentic account of their origin and subsequent services.

This defect will now be remedied, in consequence of His Majesty having been pleased to command, that every Regiment shall in future keep a full and ample record of its services at home and abroad.

From the materials thus collected, the country will henceforth derive information as to the difficulties and privations which chequer the career of those who embrace the military profession. In Great Britain, where so large a number of persons are devoted to the active concerns of agriculture, manufactures, and commerce, and where these pursuits have, for so long a period, been undisturbed by the *presence of war*, which few other countries have escaped, comparatively little is known of the vicissitudes of active service, and of the casualties of climate, to which, even during peace, the British Troops are exposed in every part of the globe, with little or no interval of repose.

In their tranquil enjoyment of the blessings which the country derives from the industry and the enterprise of the agriculturist and the trader, its happy inhabitants may be supposed not often to reflect on the perilous duties of the soldier and the sailor,—on their sufferings,—and on the sacrifice of valuable life, by which so many national benefits are obtained and preserved.

The conduct of the British Troops, their valour, and endurance, have shone conspicuously under great and trying difficulties; and their character has been established in Continental warfare by the irresistible spirit with which they have effected debarkations in spite of the most formidable opposition, and by the gallantry and steadiness with which they have maintained their advantages against superior numbers.

In the official Reports made by the respective Commanders, ample justice has generally been done to the gallant exertions of the Corps employed; but the details of their services, and of acts of individual bravery, can only be fully given in the Annals of the various Regiments.

These Records are now preparing for publication, under His Majesty's special authority, by Mr. RICHARD CANNON, Principal Clerk of the Adjutant-General's Office; and while the perusal of them cannot fail to be useful and interesting to military men of every rank, it is considered that they will also afford entertainment and information to the general reader,

particularly to those who may have served in the Army, or who have relatives in the Service.

There exists in the breasts of most of those who have served, or are serving, in the Army, an *Esprit de Corps*—an attachment to every thing belonging to their Regiment; to such persons a narrative of the services of their own Corps cannot fail to prove interesting. Authentic accounts of the actions of the great,—the valiant,—the loyal, have always been of paramount interest with a brave and civilised people. Great Britain has produced a race of heroes who, in moments of danger and terror, have stood, "firm as the rocks of their native shore;" and when half the World has been arrayed against them, they have fought the battles of their Country with unshaken fortitude. It is presumed that a record of achievements in war,—victories so complete and surprising, gained by our countrymen,—our brothers—our fellow-citizens in arms,—a record which revives the memory of the brave, and brings their gallant deeds before us, will certainly prove acceptable to the public.

Biographical memoirs of the Colonels and other distinguished Officers, will be introduced in the Records of their respective Regiments, and the Honorary Distinctions which have, from time to time, been conferred upon each Regiment, as testifying the value and importance of its services, will be faithfully set forth.

As a convenient mode of Publication, the Record of each Regiment will be printed in a distinct number, so that when the whole shall be completed, the Parts may be bound up in numerical succession.

INTRODUCTION.

The ancient Armies of England were composed of Horse and Foot; but the feudal troops established by William the Conqueror in 1086, consisted almost entirely of Horse. Under the feudal system, every holder of land amounting to what was termed a "knight's fee," was required to provide a charger, a coat of mail, a helmet, a shield, and a lance, and to serve the Crown a period of forty days in each year at his own expense; and the great landholders had to provide armed men in proportion to the extent of their estates; consequently the ranks of the feudal Cavalry were completed with men of property, and the vassals and tenants of the great barons, who led their dependents to the field in person.

In the succeeding reigns the Cavalry of the Army was composed of Knights (or men at arms) and Hobiliers (or horsemen of inferior degree); and the Infantry of spear and battle-axe men, cross-bowmen, and archers. The Knights wore armour on every part of the body, and their weapons were a lance, a sword, and a small dagger. The Hobiliers were accoutred and armed for the light and less important services of war, and were not considered qualified for a charge in line. Mounted Archers[1] were also introduced, and the English nation eventually became pre-eminent in the use of the bow.

About the time of Queen Mary the appellation of "*Men at Arms*" was changed to that of "*Spears* and *Launces*." The introduction of fire-arms ultimately occasioned the lance to fall into disuse, and the title of the Horsemen of the first degree was changed to "*Cuirassiers*." The Cuirassiers were armed *cap-à-pié*, and their weapons were a sword with a straight narrow blade and sharp point, and a pair of large pistols, called petrenels; and the Hobiliers carried carbines. The Infantry carried pikes, matchlocks, and swords. The introduction of fire-arms occasioned the formation of regiments armed and equipped as infantry, but mounted on small horses for the sake of expedition of movement, and these were styled "*Dragoons*;" a small portion of the military force of the kingdom, however, consisted of this description of troops.

The formation of the present Army commenced after the Restoration in 1660, with the establishment of regular corps of Horse and Foot; the Horsemen were cuirassiers, but only wore armour on the head and body; and the Foot were pike-men and musketeers. The arms which each description of force carried, are described in the following extract from the "Regulations of King Charles II.," dated 5th May, 1663:—

"Each Horseman to have for his defensive armes, back, breast, and pot; and for his offensive armes, a sword, and a case of pistolls, the barrels whereof are not to be und^r. foorteen inches in length; and each Trooper of Our Guards to have a carbine, besides the aforesaid armes. And the Foote to have each souldier a sword, and each pikeman a pike of 16 foote long and not und^r.; and each musqueteer a musquet, with a collar of bandaliers, the barrels of which musquet to be about foor foote long, and to conteine a bullet, foorteen of which shall weigh a pound weight[2]."

The ranks of the Troops of Horse were at this period composed of men of some property—generally the sons of substantial yeomen: the young men received as recruits provided their own horses, and they were placed on a rate of pay sufficient to give them a respectable station in society.

On the breaking out of the war with Holland, in the spring of 1672, a Regiment of Dragoons was raised[3]; the Dragoons were placed on a lower rate of pay than the Horse; and the Regiment was armed similar to the Infantry, excepting that a limited number of the men carried halberds instead of pikes, and the others muskets and bayonets; and a few men in each Troop had pistols; as appears by a warrant dated the 2nd of April, 1672, of which the following is an extract:—

"Charles R.

"Our will and pleasure is, that a Regiment of Dragoones which we have established and ordered to be raised, in twelve Troopes of fourscore in each beside officers, who are to be under the command of Our most deare and most intirely beloved Cousin Prince Rupert, shall be armed out of Our stoares remaining within Our office of the Ordinance, as followeth; that is to say, three corporalls, two serjeants, the gentlemen at

armes, and twelve souldiers of each of the said twelve Troopes, are to have and carry each of them one halbard, and one case of pistolls with holsters; and the rest of the souldiers of the several Troopes aforesaid, are to have and to carry each of them one match-locke musquet, with a collar of bandaliers, and also to have and to carry one bayonet[4], or great knife. That each lieutenant have and carry one partizan; and that two drums be delivered out for each Troope of the said Regiment[5]."

Several regiments of Horse and Dragoons were raised in the first year of the reign of King James II.; and the horsemen carried a short carbine[6] in addition to the sword and pair of pistols: and in a Regulation dated the 21st of February, 1687, the arms of the Dragoons at that period are commanded to be as follow:—

"The Dragoons to have snaphanse musquets, strapt, with bright barrels of three foote eight inches long, cartouch-boxes, bayonetts, granado pouches, bucketts, and hammer-hatchetts."

After several years' experience, little advantage was found to accrue from having Cavalry Regiments formed almost exclusively for engaging the enemy on foot; and, the Horse having laid aside their armour, the arms and equipment of Horse and Dragoons were so nearly assimilated, that there remained little distinction besides the name and rate of pay. The introduction of improvements into the mounting, arming, and equipment of Dragoons rendered them competent to the performance of every description of service required of Cavalry; and, while the long musket and bayonet were retained, to enable them to act as Infantry, if necessary, they were found to be equally efficient, and of equal value to the nation, as Cavalry, with the Regiments of Horse.

In the several augmentations made to the regular Army after the early part of the reign of Queen Anne, no new Regiments of Horse were raised for permanent service; and in 1746 King George II. reduced three of the old Regiments of Horse to the quality and pay of Dragoons; at the same time, His Majesty gave them the title of First, Second, and Third Regiments of *Dragoon Guards*: and in 1788 the same alteration was made in the

remaining four Regiments of Horse, which then became the Fourth, Fifth, Sixth, and Seventh Regiments of *Dragoon Guards*.

At present there are only three Regiments which are styled *Horse* in the British Army, namely, the two Regiments of Life Guards, and the Royal Regiment of Horse Guards, to whom cuirasses have recently been restored. The other Cavalry Regiments consist of Dragoon Guards, Heavy and Light Dragoons, Hussars, and Lancers; and although the long musket and bayonet have been laid aside by the whole of the Cavalry, and the Regiments are armed and equipped on the principle of the old Horse (excepting the cuirass), they continue to be styled Dragoons.

The old Regiments of Horse formed a highly respectable and efficient portion of the Army, and it is found, on perusing the histories of the various campaigns in which they have been engaged, that they have, on all occasions, maintained a high character for steadiness and discipline, as well as for bravery in action. They were formerly mounted on horses of superior weight and physical power, and few troops could withstand a well-directed charge of the celebrated British Horse. The records of these corps embrace a period of 150 years—a period eventful in history, and abounding in instances of heroism displayed by the British troops when danger has threatened the nation,—a period in which these Regiments have numbered in their ranks men of loyalty, valour, and good conduct, worthy of imitation.

Since the Regiments of Horse were formed into Dragoon Guards, additional improvements have been introduced into the constitution of the several corps; and the superior description of horses now bred in the United Kingdom enables the commanding officers to remount their regiments with such excellent horses, that, whilst sufficient weight has been retained for a powerful charge in line, a lightness has been acquired which renders them available for every description of service incident to modern warfare.

The orderly conduct of these Regiments in quarters has gained the confidence and esteem of the respectable inhabitants of the various parts

11

of the United Kingdom in which they have been stationed; their promptitude and alacrity in attending to the requisitions of the magistrates in periods of excitement, and the temper, patience, and forbearance which they have evinced when subjected to great provocation, insult, and violence from the misguided populace, prove the value of these troops to the Crown, and to the Government of the country, and justify the reliance which is reposed on them.

FOOTNOTES:

[1] In the 14th year of the reign of Edward IV. a small force was established in Ireland by Parliament, consisting of 120 Archers on horseback, 40 Horsemen, and 40 Pages.

[2] Military Papers, State Paper Office.

[3] This Regiment was disbanded after the Peace in 1674.

[4] This appears to be the first introduction of *bayonets* into the English Army.

[5] State Paper Office.

[6] The first issue of carbines to the regular Horse appears to have taken place in 1678; the Life Guards, however, carried carbines from their formation in 1660.—Vide the 'Historical Record of the Life Guards.'

HISTORICAL RECORD OF THE FIFTH,
OR PRINCESS CHARLOTTE OF WALES'S REGIMENT OF DRAGOON GUARDS.

1685

In the early periods of the history of this country a standing army was unknown; but as the kingdom increased in arts, sciences, and manufactures, and as national institutions, established upon sound principles, assumed an important character, a regularly organized military force was found necessary to protect the interests of society, and to guard colonial possessions; and when the other nations of Europe have from time to time augmented their standing armies, it has been found necessary to make similar additions to the regular force of Great Britain. After the Restoration in 1660, the army of the Commonwealth was disbanded, and a body of household troops, with a few garrison companies, were considered sufficient; but the acquisition of additional possessions, the ambitious designs of foreign potentates, and internal commotions in the

kingdom, have occasioned numerous additions to be made to the regular army. It was one of the last mentioned causes, which, in the year 1685, gave rise to the formation of the corps which is the subject of this memoir, and which now bears the title of the FIFTH, OR PRINCESS CHARLOTTE OF WALES'S REGIMENT OF DRAGOON GUARDS.

A difference in religious views and opinions has often occasioned long and sanguinary wars; and the accession of a Roman Catholic Prince (James II.) to the throne of Great Britain, was an event so little congenial to the feelings of a Protestant people, that James Duke of Monmouth (natural son of King Charles II.) was induced, by the persuasions of men who were disaffected to the existing government, to make a daring attempt to dethrone his uncle, and to gain the sovereignty of the kingdom. This event occurring at a time when the first feelings of alarm at the appearance of a Papist on the throne had subsided, and before the King had made any serious attack on the constitution or established religion, the people were not prepared to throw off their allegiance to their sovereign; consequently, while a few thousands of disaffected persons joined the standard of rebellion, much greater numbers arrayed themselves under the banners of royalty. Many noblemen and gentlemen exerted themselves in raising forces for the King; and it is stated in the public records, that a number of the respectable yeomen and others who volunteered their services in the royal cause, were incorporated into a troop of horse by Charles Earl of Shrewsbury, at Litchfield; another troop of horse was raised by Francis Lord Brudenel, at Kingston upon Thames; a third by Sir Thomas Grosvenor, at Chester; a fourth by Roger Pope, Esq., in the vicinity of Bridgnorth; a fifth by Mr. Francis Spalding, at Bristol; and a sixth by the Honourable John D'Arcy, (guidon of the second troop, now second regiment of Life Guards,) in London. These formed part of an extensive body of troops raised in a few weeks; but the rebellion was suppressed by the old corps which the King had in his service, without the aid of the new levies. His Majesty, however, looking forward to the commotions which would probably follow the execution

of the attacks he was urged by his jesuitical councillors to make on the established religion and laws, resolved to retain a considerable portion of the newly-raised forces in his service; and these six troops of horse were, on the 29th of July, 1685, constituted a regiment of CUIRASSIERS, of which the EARL OF SHREWSBURY was appointed Colonel, the Honourable John D'Arcy Lieutenant-Colonel, and John Skelton, Esq., Major. This regiment ranked at that period as SEVENTH HORSE; and is now the FIFTH DRAGOON GUARDS.

The uniform and equipment of this corps, like that of the other regiments of horse, were hats, long scarlet coats, jacked-leather boots, cuirasses, iron head pieces, swords, pair of pistols, and short carbines. Each corps had a distinguishing colour, then called its regimental *livery*, and now styled its *facing*, and the distinguishing colour of SHREWSBURY'S CUIRASSIERS was *buff*; the men had their coats lined with buff shalloon, and their waistcoats, breeches, ribands in their hats, and horse furniture, were of the same colour.

Soon after its formation the regiment marched into quarters near Hounslow, and experienced officers were appointed to teach the men the established military exercises; they formed two squadrons, three troops in a squadron; but each troop had a standard of buff-silk damask; and these loyal cavaliers, being mounted on strong horses, had not only a warlike appearance, but they were well calculated for a charge in line where weight and physical power were necessary. The Cuirassiers had succeeded the ancient Lancers (or Launces), formerly the highest class of military force in Europe, and celebrated for valour, prowess, and feats of chivalry. The Lancers were armed *cap à pié*, but the lance having, to a great extent, been laid aside before the middle of the seventeenth century, helmets, and armour on the limbs, were also discontinued soon afterwards. The regiments of Horse, having succeeded the ancient Lancers, were held in high estimation; and in the succeeding reigns they acquired great celebrity.

After having been twice reviewed by King James II. on Hounslow Heath, the regiment marched into quarters in Warwickshire, where it passed several months.

The King, having acquired some practical knowledge of military service in the civil war in France, and in the Netherlands, under Marshals Turenne and the Prince of Condé, established several useful regulations for the preservation of order and discipline in his army; two experienced officers, Sir John Lanier and Sir John Fenwick, were appointed Inspecting Generals of Cavalry; and the first half-yearly inspection of this regiment was made by Brigadier-General Sir John Fenwick, of the Life Guards, in its quarters in Warwickshire.

1686

While in these quarters, its establishment was fixed, by a royal warrant dated the 1st of January, 1686, at the following numbers:—

THE EARL OF SHREWSBURY'S REGIMENT OF HORSE.

FIELD AND STAFF-OFFICERS.	Per Diem.		
	£.	s.	d.
The Colonel, *as Colonel*	0	12	0
Lieutenant-Colonel, *as Lieut.-Colonel*	0	8	0
The Major (*who has no troop*), for himself, horses, and servants. }	1	0	0
Adjutant	0	5	0
Chaplaine	0	6	8
Chirurgeon iv^s per day, and j horse to carry his chest, ij^s per day }	0	6	0
A Kettle-Drummer to the Colonel's troop.	0	3	0
	3	0	8

THE COLONEL'S TROOP.

	Per Diem.		
The Colonel, *as Captaine* x^s per day, and ij horses each at ij^s per day }	0	14	0
Lievtenant vi^s, and ij horses, each at ij^s	0	10	0
Cornett v^s, and ij horses, each at ij^s	0	9	0
Quarter-Master iv^s, and i horse, at ij^s	0	6	0
Three Corporals, each at iij^s per day	0	9	0
Two Trumpeters, each at ij^s viii^d	0	5	4
Forty Private Soldiers, each at ij^s vi^d per day.	5	0	0
	7	13	4
FIVE TROOPS MORE, of the same numbers, and at the same rates of pay }	38	6	8

as the Colonel's troop			
TOTAL FOR THIS REGIMENT PER DIEM	49	0	8
PER ANNUM £17,897. 3s. 4d.			

The following officers were at this period holding commissions in the regiment:—

Troop.	Captains.	Lieutenants.	Cornets.
1st.	Earl of Shrewsbury (Col.)	John Grosvenor	George Kellum.
2d.	John Coy, (Lieut.-Col.)	James Bringfield	Hon. W. Brudenel.
3d.	Sir Thomas Grosvenor	Henry Grosvenor	James Williamson.
4th.	Roger Pope	Thomas Griffiths	Guy Forster.
5th.	Francis Spalding	Thomas Doughty	William Rowley.
6th.	Charles Orme	Thomas Manning	Ralph Pope.

John Skelton	Major.
Samuel Bowles	Chaplain.
James Arden	Surgeon.
George Briscoe	Adjutant.

The EARL OF SHREWSBURY'S CUIRASSIERS were withdrawn from their country quarters in the summer of this year, and were encamped with

other forces on Hounslow Heath; where they were practised in military evolutions, under the direction of Lieutenant-Generals the Earls of Craven, Feversham, and Dumbarton; and were several times reviewed by King James II.: in August they struck their tents and marched to Buckingham and Wendover.

1687

The King, being surrounded by Roman Catholic priests, soon gave indication of his designs against the reformed religion; the Earl of Shrewsbury, who was a stanch Protestant, resigned his commission, and afterwards proceeded to Holland and joined the Prince of Orange, to whom the nation began to look for deliverance from popish tyranny. His Majesty appointed, in January, 1687, Marmaduke Lord Langdale, to the Colonelcy of the regiment, who was succeeded in the following month by the HONOURABLE RICHARD HAMILTON, a Roman Catholic officer, from the Colonelcy of a regiment of dragoons in Ireland.

1688

From this period until that great national event, the Revolution in 1688, few circumstances occurred, in which Hamilton's regiment was particularly concerned, worthy of being recorded in this memoir. It was encamped on Hounslow Heath in the summer of 1687, and also in that of 1688; and its Colonel being a Papist, the attempt made by the King to introduce officers and soldiers of that religion into the army, would, doubtless, meet with no obstruction in this corps. The majority of the officers and men were, however, firmly attached to the Protestant cause.

The King had raised and equipped a fine army for the purpose of making it subservient to his insidious designs; but the troops proved faithful to the interests of their country and religion, and an association of officers was secretly formed at the camp on Hounslow Heath, in favour of the Prince of Orange, who was preparing an army to invade England and to rescue the kingdom from the power of the Papists.

Information having been received of the designs of the Prince of Orange, HAMILTON'S CUIRASSIERS were ordered to Ipswich, where the Earl of

Arran's regiment (now Fourth Dragoon Guards), and the Queen's (now Third) Dragoons, commanded by Colonel Alexander Cannon, were assembled under the orders of Major-General Sir John Lanier, to preserve Landguard Fort, and to prevent the Prince landing there; and two regiments of horse and one of dragoons were stationed at Colchester to support this force, if necessary. Sir John Lanier is stated by King James, in his memoirs, to have been one of the associated officers, and to have resolved to seize on the Earl of Arran, and Colonels Hamilton and Cannon, and to have joined the Prince with the three regiments; but this arrangement, in which King James states, in his memoirs, most of the officers had agreed to co-operate, was rendered void by his Highness landing at Torbay.

HAMILTON'S CUIRASSIERS were afterwards ordered to march to the metropolis, and from thence to Salisbury; but a general defection appearing in the army, the King fled to France; the Prince of Orange ordered the regiment to march to Fenny Stratford, and its Colonel, the Honourable Richard Hamilton, was confined in the Tower of London, for holding a commission for which he was disqualified by law, he being a Papist.

On the 31st of December, 1688, the Prince of Orange conferred the Colonelcy of the regiment on the Lieutenant-Colonel, John Coy; and during the eight succeeding years it bore the title of COY'S HORSE, or CUIRASSIERS.

All the Papists having been dismissed, the regiment received a draft of one hundred men and horses from the Marquis of Miremont's regiment of horse,—a corps which had been recently raised, and was now disbanded.

1689

These events were followed by the accession of William and Mary, the Prince and Princess of Orange, to the throne; and the first duty in which the regiment was called upon to engage under the new dynasty, was the patrolling of the public roads to prevent highway robberies, which, owing

to the commotions recently experienced in society, had become very frequent. It also furnished a detachment to protect the King's herd of deer in the Forest of Dean against the depredations of organized bands of deer-stealers.

From these duties COY'S HORSE were soon relieved to engage in military operations in Ireland, which country had become the theatre of intestine war. The Papists were in arms in favour of King James, who had arrived in Ireland with a body of troops from France; and, following that system of cruelty which has invariably been practised when religion has been the subject of contention, the hapless Protestants, being the weaker party, had been made to feel the full weight of Catholic vengeance. Many of the Protestants, particularly in Inniskilling and Londonderry, had taken arms. King William sent a body of troops under Duke Schomberg to their aid, and COY'S HORSE embarked at Highlake, in Cheshire, in the middle of August, 1689, for the same service.

After landing at Belfast, the regiment was employed in covering the siege of *Carrickfergus*, and had its post in the lines before the town. This place having surrendered on the 28th of August, a detachment of the regiment, commanded by Captain Sir William Russel, escorted the garrison, consisting of two regiments of foot, "all stout fellows, but ill clothed," the first stage from the town; and such cruelties had been practised by the Papists, that, according to Story, who was an eye-witness, the troopers experienced some difficulty in preserving the Catholic soldiers from being torn to pieces by the country people, who were stimulated to revenge by the remembrance of past injuries.

The regiment afterwards advanced with the army towards Newry, where a party of the enemy was assembled, who, on the approach of the English, set fire to the town, and retreated over the mountains to Dundalk. The English passed the mountains on the following day, when the enemy quitted Dundalk and retired to Atherdee, where the main body of King James's army was assembled.

Marshal Duke Schomberg, finding Dundalk to be a strong situation, with a convenient harbour for obtaining supplies from England, and knowing that the enemy's army was more than double his own in numbers, formed an intrenched camp, where he resolved to continue during the remainder of the campaign; but the ground where the troops were encamped being low, and the weather proving wet, this injudicious choice of situation proved so fatal to his army, that the infantry corps lost half their men from disease. COY'S HORSE remained at Dundalk upwards of a month, and afterwards proceeded to Carlingford for the convenience of forage. During the winter, detached parties had frequent encounters with the bands of armed Papists who prowled the country, committing every description of outrage; and an out-guard of the regiment, posted in the pass of Newry, was sharply engaged with a party of the enemy, who attempted to force the pass, but were repulsed with loss, the gallant English Cuirassiers proving more than a match for their antagonists.

1690

In June, 1690, King William arrived in Ireland to command the army in person, and the regiment was now called upon to serve under the eye of its sovereign. This circumstance is said to have given rise to a laudable feeling of emulation in all ranks of the army, and the troopers longed for an opportunity to distinguish themselves in presence of their King. The desired opportunity soon occurred; the King, advancing up to the banks of the *Boyne*, found the enemy in position on the opposite side of the river, and the troops prepared for battle. This regiment was with His Majesty on the evening preceding the battle, while reconnoitring the enemy's position, and was exposed to a cannonade, on which occasion the King was wounded in the shoulder, and the regiment had three men and nine horses killed.

Early on the 1st of July, as the rays of morning-light shed their lustre on the camp, the English and Dutch troops appeared in motion, every man displaying a green branch in his hat; and soon the columns were seen advancing towards the Boyne, their glittering arms, waving plumes, and

floating banners, exhibiting all the pomp of war: the French and Irish stood to their arms and prepared to defend their post. COY'S HORSE, forming part of the cavalry of the right wing, were in the column which forded the river near Slane Bridge; some opposition was made by a regiment of Irish dragoons, which was attacked, and its commanding officer and about 70 men killed. After passing the river, the troops advanced through large corn-fields, crossed several deep ditches, and overcoming every obstacle with an ardour which bespoke the valour and confidence which glowed in every breast, the enemy's left wing was dismayed and retreated towards Duleck. COY'S HORSE were amongst the squadrons which galloped forward in pursuit, and charging the Irish foot, cut them down with a great slaughter. While these events were transpiring on the right, King William passed the river with the main body of his forces: the enemy was overpowered at every point, and His Majesty stood triumphant on the field of battle. King James fled to Dublin, and afterwards to France, and was followed by the French troops; but the Irish Papists resolved to maintain his cause to the last extremity.

COY'S HORSE advanced with King William to Dublin, and were afterwards with the army before *Limerick*, during the unsuccessful siege of that place, when His Majesty returned to England, the regiment went into quarters near Cork.

1691

In the depth of the winter an incursion into the enemy's cantonments was resolved upon; and the regiment having joined the forces selected for that service, advanced, on the 31st of December, into the county of Kerry. On arriving near Brewsterfield, the van-guard, consisting of a troop of this regiment and one of Eppinger's Dragoons, encountered a party of 160 of the enemy's cavalry. COY'S HORSE and the dragoons instantly drew their swords, and advanced to charge their opponents, who fled in a panic. Continuing its route, the detachment took a number of prisoners, also drove seven troops of Irish horse and twenty-one of dragoons from Tralee, and afterwards returned to its quarters.

When the army took the field in the summer of 1691, COY'S HORSE were left in dispersed quarters in the county of Cork to overawe the disaffected, and to check the depredations of the bands of Papists, whose proceedings were very injurious to the Protestants; the regiment was, consequently, not at the battle of Aghrim, but it afterwards joined the army near *Limerick*, and was employed in the siege of that place.

On the 16th of September, a squadron of the regiment, with a strong party of dragoons and infantry, crossed the Shannon by a pontoon bridge before break of day, surprised and defeated a body of the enemy, and captured a standard; also surprised the troops in the camp near the town, and forced them to make a precipitate flight to the mountains. On the 24th of the same month, a cessation of hostilities took place, which ended in a treaty, and the authority of King James was extinguished in Ireland.

1692

1693

The regiment, having thus performed its part in reducing Ireland to submission to the authority of King William, embarked at Belfast in the beginning of 1692, and after its arrival in England it was quartered at Huntingdon, Chester, and St. Ives; from whence it proceeded to the vicinity of London, and, for a short time, assisted the Life Guards in performing the escort duty for the royal family. It was, however, allowed but a short period of home service before it was called upon to take the field against a foreign enemy.

King William was engaged in a war to restrain the ambitious designs of Louis XIV. of France, who sought to become the dictator of Europe and the destroyer of the reformed religion. After the severe loss sustained by the confederates at the battle of Landen, in 1693, the British monarch gave orders for Colonel Coy to proceed with his regiment of horse to the Netherlands, and to join the army in that country.

1694

On its arrival in Flanders, the regiment was placed in quarters at Ghent; from whence it marched to Tirlemont, and, joining the army commanded

by King William in person, took part in the operations of the long and toilsome campaign of 1694, but was not engaged in any action of importance.

1695

In the following year the regiment formed part of the covering army during the siege of the strong and important fortress of *Namur*, which was superintended by King William in person. Two magnificent armies confronted each other, and manœuvred, the one to prevent, and the other to ensure, the capture of this strong fortress; and it was eventually taken by the forces commanded by His Britannic Majesty. About a month after the surrender of the castle of Namur, the regiment marched into quarters at Ghent.

1696

King William reviewed the regiment near Ghent, in May, 1696, and expressed his approbation of its appearance. During this summer it formed part of the army of Flanders, under the orders of the veteran Prince of Vaudemont, and was encamped for several months on the canal between Ghent and Bruges, and its services were limited to defensive measures for the preservation of these two places, and the maritime towns of Flanders from the attacks of the enemy. On the 4th of October, the regiment returned to its former station at Ghent.

1697

From Ghent the regiment marched in May, 1697, to join the army of Brabant, and was encamped a short time at St. Quintin Linneck. The French besieged the town of Aeth; and a body of troops was sent out, under Brigadier-General Lumley, to make a reconnoissance towards *Enghien*, with the view of attacking the French army and raising the siege. A detachment of COY'S HORSE, commanded by Sir William Russel, formed the advance-guard on this occasion; and when on the march, he encountered a party of French hussars, carabiniers, and dragoons. Upon notice of the approach of the enemy, the main body of the British force concealed itself in the wood, and formed an ambush; and the advance-

guard retiring, the French advanced boldly forward, and were nearly every man killed or taken prisoner.

The design of relieving Aeth was afterwards laid aside; King William retired, and subsequently took up a position before Brussels.

Colonel John Coy having obtained His Majesty's permission to dispose of the Colonelcy of the regiment to CHARLES EARL OF ARRAN,[7] brother of the Duke of Ormond, his lordship was appointed to the regiment on the 1st of July, 1697; and during the succeeding five years it was styled ARRAN'S HORSE.

King William, after waging war for the good of Europe a period of nine years, had the satisfaction of seeing his endeavours succeeded by a treaty of peace, which was signed at Ryswick in September of this year.

1698

Shortly after this event, ARRAN'S HORSE were ordered to return to England, where they arrived in January, 1698, and were quartered at Coventry, Daventry, and Towcester.

1699

1700

The army in England having been reduced by the House of Commons to the low establishment of seven thousand men, King William was under the necessity of disbanding several corps, and of sending others to Ireland. This regiment was one of the corps selected to proceed to Ireland, where it arrived in the summer of 1700, and its numbers were reduced to thirty-six private men per troop.

1701

The repose granted to Europe by the treaty of Ryswick was, however, of short duration. Louis XIV. of France, procured the accession of his grandson, the Duke of Anjou, to the throne of Spain; this virtual union of two powerful states, rekindled the flame of war; and the EARL OF ARRAN'S regiment was one of the cavalry corps ordered to be augmented to fifty-seven private men per troop, and held in readiness to proceed on foreign service; but so great was the difficulty experienced in raising an

army of sufficient numbers to meet the exigence of the nation on this sudden emergency, that only three troops of the regiment could, in the first instance, be spared from Ireland.

1702

These three troops landed at Highlake, in Cheshire, in the beginning of March, 1702, and marching to London, embarked in transports on the river Thames in the beginning of April, and sailed for Holland.

The decease of King William, who might justly be styled the protector of the reformed religion, and the accession of Queen Anne, produced no alteration in the foreign policy of the British court. The war was prosecuted with vigour, and the three troops of ARRAN'S HORSE, forming one squadron, were attached to Brigadier-General Wood's regiment (now Third Dragoon Guards), and served the campaign of this year under the Earl of Marlborough. The British horse, had, however no opportunity of signalizing themselves in action this year; their services being limited to out-post duty, and covering the sieges of *Venloo, Ruremonde, Stevenswaert*, and the famous city of *Liege*, which fortresses were captured by the British commander.

1703

The Earl of Arran having been promoted to the Colonelcy of the third troop of Life Guards, Queen Anne conferred the command of the regiment on BRIGADIER-GENERAL CADOGAN (afterwards EARL CADOGAN), from the Sixth, or Inniskilling Dragoons, by commission, dated the 2d of March, 1703.

The three troops of the regiment on foreign service, now bearing the title of CADOGAN'S HORSE, continued to serve throughout the campaign of this year with Brigadier-General Wood's regiment. In a slight skirmish near *Haneff*, in the beginning of June, a small detachment evinced the martial spirit and valour of British troopers; and in the various movements of the army before the enemy, the national character was fully sustained. The French commanders avoided an engagement, and after

covering the sieges of *Huy* and *Limburg*, CADOGAN'S HORSE went into quarters for the winter in Holland.

1704

In the beginning of the following year the other three troops of the regiment were withdrawn from Ireland, and after occupying quarters a short time at Northampton, embarked (4th April, 1704) for Holland.

The six troops were thus united in time for the whole regiment to take part in the glorious exploits of the campaign of 1704, in which that noble ardour and chivalric spirit which has raised Britain to its present exalted station among the nations of Europe, were displayed by the army under the Duke of Marlborough in a signal manner. Confidence in the commander has always given additional life and vigour to innate valour, and the troops having already proved the military virtues of their leader, the great Marlborough was enabled to march his forces from the ocean to the Danube, and to gain new honours in the heart of Germany.

This enterprise was undertaken in consequence of the armies of France and Bavaria having united against the Emperor of Germany, and the British general advanced to the aid of the house of Austria, which was thus menaced by a force which it was unable to withstand. Quitting the territory of the Dutch republic the army crossed the Rhine, and traversed the various states of Germany with a degree of order and regularity which bespoke a high state of discipline, united with excellent arrangements, while the nations of Europe gazed with astonishment at the undertaking.

Having arrived at the theatre of war and joined the Imperial army, the first action of importance was the attack of a body of French and Bavarians commanded by the Count d'Arco, at their entrenched camp on the lofty heights of *Schellenberg*, on the 2d of July. On this occasion the cavalry supported the attacks of the infantry, and when the enemy was forced from the entrenchments, the brilliant charge of the English horse, and Royal Scots Dragoons (the Greys) completed the overthrow; the hostile army lost its colours, cannon, and baggage, and numbers of French and Bavarians fell beneath the conquering sabres of the British horsemen,

who chased their adversaries to the banks of the Danube, and captured many prisoners. CADOGAN'S HORSE were commanded on this occasion by Lieutenant-Colonel George Kellum, and had Major Napier,[8] Lieutenant Tettefall, and several private men wounded; and sustained a serious loss in troop horses, from having been exposed to a heavy cannonade: their Colonel, Brigadier-General Cadogan, was also wounded.

This action was the precursor of a greater overthrow to the forces of the enemy, who made efforts to retrieve his affairs; new armies and new generals appeared; but these only served to augment the splendour of victory, and to enhance the value of the conquerors in the estimation of the world. The action was fought in the valley of the Danube, near the village of *Blenheim*, on the 13th of August, and the English horsemen, who during the two preceding campaigns had panted for an opportunity to signalize themselves, had a fair field in which to display their valour and prowess, and they gave undeniable proofs of their good qualities. The Gallo-Bavarian army was destroyed; its commander, Marshal Tallard, and many entire battalions and squadrons were made prisoners of war; and the field of battle was literally covered with trophies.

The victory was most complete and decisive, and it was not gained over new levies; but over an army of veterans fully instructed in the art of war,—select troops flushed with former successes, and commanded by generals of great bravery and experience.[9] This regiment had only one officer (Lieutenant Groubere) killed; its loss in non-commissioned officers and private men has not been recorded.

The regiment took part in the subsequent operations of the main army; and after covering the siege of *Laudan*, it marched back to Holland for winter quarters.

1705

In the following summer the regiment marched with the army through the Duchy of Juliers, and crossed the Moselle and the Saar, in order to carry on the war in Alsace; but the Duke of Marlborough, being disappointed

of the promised co-operation of the Imperialists, marched back to the Netherlands.

The French had, with much labour and art, constructed a line of fortifications of many miles extent to cover their recently acquired territory in the Spanish Netherlands, and CADOGAN'S HORSE having been selected to form part of the division to be employed in forcing these lines, had an opportunity of distinguishing themselves, and their valour shone forth with as bright a lustre as in any of the heroes in the ancient days of chivalry. The British commander, having by skilful movements succeeded in drawing the main body of the French army from the point selected for the attack, forced the lines at *Helixem* and *Neer-Hespen* at day-break on the morning of the 18th of July, and the pioneers levelled a space for the cavalry to pass over; but scarcely had the British horse passed the barriers, when the Marquis d'Allegre appeared with fifty squadrons of cavalry and twenty battalions of infantry to drive back the British forces. The sun had risen, and the French army was in full march to oppose this sudden attack on their lines; hence every moment was of importance, and a sharp fire of musketry having forced the enemy from a hollow way, the Duke of Marlborough ordered forward his heavy cavalry to charge the hostile horsemen. The two squadrons of this regiment led the attack with their characteristic gallantry, and were opposed to adversaries of valour and renown,—the famous Bavarian Horse Grenadier Guards. Against these celebrated antagonists CADOGAN'S HORSE advanced; the weight and power of their compact line were irresistible, and the Bavarians were broken at the first shock; but they soon rallied, and renewing the conflict with increasing ardour, gained a temporary advantage. At this critical juncture the Duke of Marlborough was separated from his troops and in imminent danger, when CADOGAN'S HORSE, exasperated at the momentary repulse, and still more so at the peril of their renowned chief, returned to the charge; the grand spectacle of two spirited corps of heavy cavalry rushing upon each other with reckless fury, was soon followed by the clash of swords and shouts of the combatants as they fought hand to

hand with sanguinary fury; but British prowess and British valour soon proved triumphant, and the Bavarians were overpowered and fled before the conquering sabres of CADOGAN'S troopers, who chased their adversaries from the field, took many prisoners, and captured *four standards*. In their flight the hostile horsemen rode over two battalions of their own foot, and these battalions were severely handled by the British horse. Finally, the enemy was routed; the Marquis d'Allegre, and many officers and men were made prisoners, and this gallant enterprise was attended with complete success.

On this occasion the regiment, which forms the subject of this memoir, gained great honour; the Duke of Marlborough observed in one of his letters,—"*Never men fought better!*" and in his public despatch he states, "*They acquitted themselves with a bravery surpassing all that could have been hoped of them.*" The author of the Annals of Queen Anne observed:—"All the troops of the confederates behaved themselves with great bravery and resolution; but among the HORSE the regiment of Brigadier CADOGAN distinguished themselves, having had the honour to charge first, which they did with that success, that they defeated four squadrons of Bavarian Guards, drove them through two battalions of their own foot, and took four standards; and this with the loss only of Lieutenant Austin and some few men killed."

The following description of the standards captured on this occasion is copied from the London Gazette.

"Nine standards of blue satin, richly embroidered with the Bavarian arms; six belonging to the Elector's own troops, and three to those of Cologne, having the following devices and mottoes."

1st. A laurel; motto, *Aut Coronari aut rumpi.*

2d. An olive-tree on a rock; motto, *Per Ardua Laurus.*

3d. A pillar reaching to the clouds; motto, *Tantum Umbra movetur.*

4th. A bear rampant; motto, *Ex Vulnere Crudelior.*

5th. A dove with a laurel branch; motto, *Uni servo fidem.*

6th. A chaos; motto, *Obstantia firmant.*

7th. A helmet with a feather on a pedestal; motto, *Ex duris Gloria.*

8th. An olive-tree shading serpents; motto, *Nocet Umbra nocenti.*

9th. A standard of the Elector's guards with the colour torn to pieces.

Four of these standards were taken by CADOGAN'S HORSE; the corps which captured the other five standards are not specified.

Brigadier-General Cadogan's Horse forcing the French Lines, 18th July, 1705:—

NOW FIFTH (THE PRINCESS CHARLOTTE OF WALES'S) REGIMENT OF DRAGOON GUARDS.

1706

After this victory the regiment was employed in several manœuvres; but it was not engaged in any action of importance until the battle of *Ramilies,* fought on Whit-Sunday, the 23d of May, 1706, when the French, Bavarians, and Spaniards, commanded by Marshal Villeroy and the Elector of Bavaria, sustained another decisive overthrow, and CADOGAN'S HORSE acquired new laurels in the contest. On this occasion the English cavalry were kept in reserve near the heights of Foulz until towards the

close of the action, when they were brought forward, and the weight and fury of the charge of these heavy horsemen were irresistible; the enemy's squadrons and battalions were broken; and the British troopers,—strong men on powerful horses,—smote their antagonists to the ground with a dreadful slaughter. The victorious squadrons pursued their adversaries throughout the night, capturing officers and soldiers, colours, standards, and cannon; and thus, in a few hours, the French monarch's fine and well-appointed army was nearly annihilated, and its commanders escaped from the field with difficulty.

This glorious victory was followed by the submission of a great part of Spanish Brabant and Flanders to the house of Austria; and in a few days after the battle, this regiment was selected to form part of a detachment commanded by its Colonel, Brigadier-General Cadogan, sent from the main army, to summon *Antwerp*, which place was surrendered on the 7th of June.

The regiment was subsequently employed in the blockade of *Dendermond*, and continued before that town until its surrender on the 5th of September.

1707

During the campaigns from 1702 to 1706 the British regiments of horse had not worn cuirasses. In the preceding century armour had, as already stated, fallen, to a great extent, into disuse; several English regiments of heavy cavalry delivered their cuirasses into the Tower of London in November, 1688; but subsequently had them returned: they were, however, again placed in store after the peace of Ryswick. The French and other continental nations had continued the use of defensive armour, and it having been observed that the English heavy cavalry, though they proved victorious, frequently sustained a very serious loss in killed, they were, in order to place them on an equality with their antagonists, again supplied with cuirasses in the spring of 1707.

In the summer of this year, when the regiment took the field, it again appeared as a corps of CUIRASSIERS: the campaign was passed in manœuvring; and the French acting on the defensive, a few skirmishes between detached parties was all the fighting which took place.

1708

The following campaign was, however, distinguished by more important events. The enemy assembled an immense army, and advancing from behind their lines, gained possession of Ghent and Bruges (which places had been wrested from them in 1706), and advanced to *Oudenarde*, with the design of besieging that town. The Duke of Marlborough sent Major-General Cadogan forward with three brigades of infantry and eight squadrons of Hanoverian cavalry, and following with the main army, this movement brought on a general engagement, which was fought in the ground near the banks of the Scheldt on the 11th of July. The reputation already acquired by the British regiments of horse, occasioned them to be accounted a choice body of troops; and they were kept in reserve ready to advance at the moment when a powerful charge of heavy cavalry was likely to prove decisive. For a short time they were formed in column behind the right wing; and advancing from thence, supported the attacks of the infantry; but the enemy was overpowered, and darkness put an end

to the conflict before this compact body of CUIRASSIERS was called upon to charge.

After this victory, the Duke of Marlborough was joined by a body of Germans, under the orders of Prince Eugene of Savoy, and, to the astonishment of all Europe, these two commanders resolved to besiege the important fortress of *Lisle*. CADOGAN'S CUIRASSIERS formed part of the covering army, and the attempts of the enemy to raise the siege were all frustrated.

Six hundred waggons, laden with necessaries for the army, were advancing from Ostend towards Lisle, under an escort commanded by Major-General Webb; and the enemy having detached twenty-two thousand men to intercept this convoy, the Duke of Marlborough sent Major-General Cadogan with a body of horse to reinforce the guard, and this regiment formed part of the force sent forward. The enemy attacked the convoy in the wood of *Wynendale*, and Major-General Webb made a most skilful and gallant defence. As this regiment approached the wood, the noise of combat was heard; the squadrons galloped forward, and the moment they arrived at the scene of conflict, the French desisted, and made a precipitate retreat; and the waggons were brought in safety to the camp. The fate of Lisle depended, in a great measure, on the safe arrival of this convoy; and Major-General Webb was rewarded with the thanks of Parliament and the approbation of Queen Anne for his conduct.

The siege of *Lisle* was continued, and the enemy being unable to relieve the place, resolved to make an attack upon Brussels. The covering army, of which CADOGAN'S CUIRASSIERS formed part, was put in motion; and having forced the passage of the *Scheldt*, the Elector of Bavaria raised the siege of Brussels and retreated. The citadel of Lisle surrendered on the 9th of December, and Ghent and Bruges were also recaptured before the army entered into winter quarters.

1709

In the summer of 1709, when the siege of the strong fortress of *Tournay* was resolved upon, this was one of the regiments which first invested the

town on the 27th of June, 1709. After the capture of this place, the army advanced towards Mons, the capital of the province of Hainault, with the design of capturing that important city. The French army, commanded by Marshals Villiers and Boufflers, manœuvred to prevent the loss of Mons, and this brought on the sanguinary battle of *Malplaquet*, where the British regiments of horse encountered enemies who fought with greater spirit and obstinacy than on any former occasion during this war. This battle was fought on the 11th of September, 1709. The enemy had an advantageous position, covered by thick woods, protected by barriers of trees cut down and laid across each other, with a treble entrenchment, batteries, and pallisades; and within these formidable works were collected the choicest troops of France under commanders of renown. This post was attacked with a bravery which overcame all opposition; the woods were pierced, the obstacles were overcome, and the fortifications were trampled down. The position having been forced, the Duke of Marlborough led the British CUIRASSIERS and Prussian cavalry against the French gens d'armes, who were routed and chased from the ground; but scarcely were these squadrons overcome, when the British and Prussian horse encountered a compact line of French cavalry of the royal household, and were driven back in some disorder. The British horse soon rallied, and returning to the charge, overcame their celebrated adversaries, and the French squadrons were driven from the field. The allies were victorious, but they sustained a severe loss in killed and wounded.

CADOGAN'S HORSE were afterwards employed in covering the siege of *Mons*, which was terminated by the surrender of the place on the 20th of October.

1710

During the campaign of 1710, the regiment was employed in covering the sieges of *Douay, Bethune, Aire*, and *St. Venant*, and in protecting convoys of military stores to the besieging troops.

1711

In the summer of 1711, the imperialists, under Prince Eugene, having returned to Germany, the Duke of Marlborough confronted the French army with the forces under his orders. The French had constructed very extensive and strong lines of fortifications to cover their frontiers, and within these lines they had collected a numerous army. The Duke, by a skilful device, induced them to destroy their fort at Arleux; and then, by menacing their lines between the head of the Sanzet and Hesdin, caused them to withdraw part of their garrisons from Arras and Cambray, with the troops which guarded the lines in the direction of Arleux. In the mean time his grace was continually sending detachments towards Douay, where a considerable body of troops was assembled without attracting notice, and amongst these forces were the two squadrons of CADOGAN'S CUIRASSIERS. Having reconnoitred the lines on the 4th of August, the Duke gave orders for the troops to prepare for the attack on the following morning, and the French army prepared to receive him with eclat; but at the dead of the night, Lieutenant-General Cadogan, having advanced with great secrecy with the troops from Douay, passed the lines at the causeway of *Arleux*, which the French commander, in his anxiety to collect all the troops he could to resist the menaced attack, had left unguarded; and the main army struck its tents in the night, and marched in the same direction. When Marshal Villiers heard that his lines were passed, he was astounded. He took with him the household cavalry, and, ordering his army to follow as quickly as possible, rode with all speed, until he came within the English out-guards, and his feelings were so excited, that he was nearly surrounded by a troop of CADOGAN'S HORSE before he was conscious of danger; he had proceeded with such rapidity that the whole of his escort, except a hundred of the best mounted dragoons, was left behind; he ordered these dragoons to throw themselves into the old castle of Oisy, which was at hand, and himself and two officers of his staff escaped; but the dragoons were surrounded and made prisoners.

Having thus passed these extensive lines, which the French commander had vauntingly called Marlborough's *ne plus ultra*, his grace besieged the strong and important fortress of *Bouchain*, situate on the Scheldt, in the taking of which place, difficulties of great magnitude had to be overcome. Marshal Villiers, by a secret march, during the night of the 9th of August, gained possession of the heights of *Wavrechin*, in order to preserve the line of communication which runs from thence, through a morass between the Scheldt and the Senset, to the town of Bouchain, that he might be enabled to relieve the garrison from time to time. The Duke of Marlborough, observing the enemy at work, throwing up entrenchments on the hill, ordered Lieutenant-Generals Cadogan and Fagel to march with a body of troops, of which CADOGAN'S HORSE formed part, to dislodge the French. As the British grenadiers advanced to the attack, his grace rode forwards to reconnoitre the works on the hill; and observing that the entrenchment was a perfect bulwark, strong and lofty, and crouded with men and cannon, he gave orders for the troops to retire.

On the following day Marshal Villiers issued from the works with a hundred hussars, to observe the progress of his opponent, and encountered Lieutenant-General Cadogan, who was reconnoitering with a squadron of horse. A skirmish ensued, and four squadrons of French carabineers advanced to aid the marshal. Cadogan, being thus out-numbered, made a precipitate retreat, which occasioned the enemy to pursue with great eagerness. Meanwhile, CADOGAN'S HORSE and two other squadrons, advanced from the camp, and formed up beyond the summit of a rising ground, where they were out of the enemy's sight; and the moment the French carabineers appeared on the top of the hill, they were charged by Cadogan's squadrons with such resolution, that they were immediately broken. Marshal Villiers was in danger of being surrounded and taken prisoner, but a French brigadier-general interposed, with singular bravery, and rescued the marshal. The gallant brigadier was severely wounded and taken prisoner, and most of his men cut down by

the British CUIRASSIERS; and Marshal Villiers galloped back with his shattered squadrons with greater haste than he had advanced.

Fortifications were afterwards constructed, with a causeway through the inundations, and the communication between the town of Bouchain and the troops on the heights of Wavrechin was cut off. The siege was prosecuted with zeal and energy, and Marshal Villiers and a numerous French army were spectators of the capture of this important fortress. After the works were repaired and the place put in a state of defence, the troops were placed in winter quarters.

The splendid successes of the army commanded by the Duke of Marlborough, who never fought a battle which he did not win, nor besieged a town which he did not capture, had effected a complete revolution in the affairs of Europe, and the King of France saw his generals over-matched,—his armies beaten and dispirited,—his possessions wrested from him,—the barriers of his kingdom trampled down,—his fortresses captured, and a powerful army, with an invincible leader, ready to carry all the horrors of war into the heart of France: with his designs thus frustrated, and his kingdom thus menaced, the ambitious Louis XIV., who had thought to have dictated laws to christendom, became a negociator for peace.

1712

In the summer of 1712, while the conditions of the treaty were under consideration, the regiment again took the field, and, advancing to the frontiers of France, formed part of the army under the orders of the Duke of Ormond, and encamped at Cateau-Cambresis during the siege of *Quesnoy*.

A suspension of hostilities was soon afterwards published between the British and French, and the army retired from Cateau-Cambresis to Ghent, where the English CUIRASSIERS and several other corps were encamped for a short time, and afterwards were placed in quarters.

Political events connected with the amity which had been induced between the British and French courts, in consequence of a change of

measures; the conditions of the treaty of peace then under consideration; and the disagreement between the Duke of Marlborough and Queen Anne; occasioned Lieutenant-General Cadogan, who was a stanch Protestant and a warm advocate for the succession of the house of Hanover, to be called upon to dispose of his commission; and he was succeeded in the Colonelcy of this regiment by Lieutenant-General GEORGE KELLUM, who had been many years the Lieutenant-Colonel of the regiment, and whose commission as Colonel was dated 22nd of December, 1712.

1713

1714

The regiment, now styled KELLUM'S HORSE, was placed upon the Irish establishment in June, 1713; but it remained in comfortable quarters in Flanders until the early part of the year 1714, when it embarked for Ireland. The treaty of peace having been concluded, the troopers of this regiment could look back with triumph and exultation at their brilliant career during the late eventful and important war; and although there were circumstances connected with the conduct of their government calculated to produce painful feelings, yet, conscious of their own merit and justly acquired fame, the officers and soldiers could rejoice that, by their well-directed exertions, they had humbled the enemies of their country, the British troops had become celebrated for valour and intrepidity throughout Europe, and that the turmoil and horrors of war were succeeded by the blessings and enjoyments of peace.

1715

1716

After its arrival in Ireland, the regiment was stationed for a short time at Dublin; and having been thus removed from the scenes of conflict and bloodshed in which it had for several years been engaged, to the more pacific and easy duties of home service, the CUIRASSES were again returned into store. Ireland was not, however, in a state of internal tranquillity; the decease of Queen Anne and the accession of King George

I. were followed by great exertions on the part of the friends of the house of Stuart, who were numerous in Ireland; and when the rebellion broke out in Scotland in 1715, and extended itself to England, this event gave buoyancy to the expectations of the malcontents in Ireland. The troops in Ireland were kept in a state of constant readiness for active service; several corps embarked for England, and the fidelity of the ARMY preserved the kingdom from anarchy and papal domination; by the exertions of the troops the rebellion was suppressed, and the country restored to tranquillity.

1717

In the spring of 1717, Lieutenant-General George Kellum retired from the service, and King George I. was graciously pleased to confer the Colonelcy on the Lieutenant-Colonel, ROBERT NAPIER, who was celebrated for his conduct at the head of the regiment in several actions in the Netherlands, and was wounded in the action at Schellenberg.

About this period, the distinguishing colour, or facing of the regiment, was changed from *buff* to *green*, and it has continued of this colour to the present time (1838); its lace was also changed from *silver* to *gold*. The men having *green* waistcoats, breeches, and horse furniture, the regiment was emphatically styled the GREEN HORSE, and this appellation has been continued to the present time.

1718

1740

The regiment remained in Ireland performing a successive routine of court and country duties, at the establishment of twenty-five private men per troop, until 1740, when an augmentation of ten men per troop was made to its numbers.

After the decease of Lieutenant-General Robert Napier, King George II. conferred the Colonelcy of the regiment on Major-General Clement Neville, from the Eighth Dragoons, his commission bearing date the 6th of May, 1740.

1741

1742

1743

1744

Another war having broken out on the continent, the establishment of the regiment received a further addition of ten men per troop in 1741. In the following year a British army was sent to Flanders under Field-Marshal the Earl of Stair; but the necessity for retaining a considerable body of troops in Ireland, occasioned this regiment to remain in that country. It, however, sent a detachment of sixty men and horses to Flanders in the beginning of 1743, to complete the three regiments of horse on foreign service, and another detachment was sent in 1744.

1745

Lieutenant-General Neville died on the 5th of August, 1744, and was succeeded in the Colonelcy of the regiment by Richard Viscount Cobham, who, when Sir Richard Temple, highly distinguished himself in the wars of Queen Anne. He was removed in 1745 to the Tenth Dragoons, when His Majesty conferred the command of this regiment on Major-General Thomas Wentworth, from the Twenty-fourth Foot.

1746

When this regiment was first raised, it ranked as SEVENTH HORSE; in 1690, the Fifth regiment of Horse was disbanded in Ireland, and the Sixth Horse became Fifth, and this regiment obtained rank as SIXTH HORSE, which rank it held until December, 1746, when the First Horse,—the royal regiment of Horse Guards,—ceased to bear a number: the Second, Third, and Fourth Horse were then constituted the First, Second, and Third Dragoon Guards; and this regiment was styled the SECOND IRISH HORSE, and sometimes called the GREEN HORSE from the colour of its facings.

1747

In 1747, Major-General Thomas Wentworth died at Turin, where he was employed in a diplomatic capacity, and was succeeded in the Colonelcy of

the SECOND IRISH HORSE, by Major-General Thomas Bligh, from the Twelfth Dragoons.

1748

 1749

On the conclusion of a treaty of peace at Aix-la-Chapelle, a considerable diminution was made in the strength of the regular army, and in 1749 the establishment of the SECOND IRISH HORSE was reduced to twenty-one private men per troop.

1751

From the period of the formation of the regiment, several alterations had, from time to time, been made in the uniform and standards. The practice of having a standard to each troop had been discontinued, and one to each squadron was substituted. In 1742, King George II. caused a series of coloured engravings, representing the uniform of the several regiments of the army to be executed; and, as a few alterations had subsequently been made, a warrant was issued on the 1st of July, 1751, regulating the standards, colours, and clothing of the several regiments, from which the following particulars have been extracted relative to the SECOND IRISH HORSE:—

COATS.—Scarlet, the facings and lapels of full green; the button-holes worked with yellow, the buttons set on two and two; and a long slash pocket in each skirt.

WAISTCOATS } full green.

 BREECHES }

HATS.—Three-cornered cocked-hats, bound with yellow lace, and ornamented with a brass loop and a black cockade.

BOOTS.—Made of jacked leather.

TRUMPETERS.—Clothed in full green coats, faced and lapelled with red, and ornamented with white lace, having a red stripe down the middle: their waistcoats and breeches of red cloth.

HORSE FURNITURE of full green; the holster caps and housings having a border of broad white lace with a red worm down the centre, and

44

II
H

embroidered on a red ground, within a wreath of roses and thistles on each corner of the housings; and on the holster caps, the King's cypher and crown, with

II
H

underneath.

STANDARDS.—The first, or King's standard, to be of crimson damask, embroidered and fringed with gold; the rose and thistle conjoined, and crown over them in the centre; and underneath, His Majesty's motto, *Dieu et mon droit*: the white horse in a compartment in the first and fourth corners, and

II
H

in gold characters, on a full green ground, in a compartment in the second and third corners. The second and third standards to be of full green damask, embroidered and fringed with gold; the rank of the regiment in gold Roman characters on a crimson ground, within a wreath of roses and thistles on the same stalk, and the motto, *Vestigia nulla retrorsum*, underneath: the white horse on a red ground in the first and fourth compartments, and the rose and thistle conjoined upon a red ground in the second and third compartments.

OFFICERS to be distinguished by narrow gold lace or embroidery to the binding and button-holes of their coats; sword knots of crimson and gold in stripes; and crimson silk sashes worn over the left shoulder.

1758

1759

1760

On the 23d of October, 1758, Lieutenant-General Bligh was succeeded in the Colonelcy of the regiment by Major-General the Honourable John Waldegrave (afterwards Earl Waldegrave), who was removed to the

45

Second Dragoon Guards in the following year. The Colonelcy appears to have remained vacant from September, 1759, to November, 1760, when it was conferred by King George III. on Major-General the Honourable John Fitz-William from the Second, or Queen's Royal Regiment of Foot.

1762

Another war having commenced in 1756, between Great Britain and France, a British army was sent to Germany in 1758; the establishment of this regiment was augmented to forty-nine private men per troop; and in 1762 the order prohibiting the regiment recruiting in Ireland was rescinded.

1763

The success of the British arms in Canada, the West Indies, and Germany, was followed by a treaty of peace, and after the return of the cavalry regiments from Germany, in the beginning of 1763, the establishment of the SECOND IRISH HORSE was again reduced to twenty-one private men per troop.

1776

1783

At this low establishment the regiment continued until the breaking out of the unfortunate contest between Great Britain and her North American colonies, when an augmentation of ten private men per troop was made to its numbers. No further alteration appears to have been made until the conclusion of the war, when, the independence of the United States having been acknowledged, its establishment was reduced to its former numbers.

1788

At this establishment it continued until the spring of 1788; when King George III., having resolved to form the two troops of Life Guards and two troops of Horse Grenadier Guards into two regiments of Life Guards on a similar establishment to that of the old regiments of horse, and to reduce the four regiments of horse on the Irish establishment to the pay of dragoons, with the title of DRAGOON GUARDS, His Majesty's pleasure

was communicated to the regiments in Ireland, in a General Order dated the 14th of February, 1788; and the SECOND IRISH HORSE was thus constituted the FIFTH DRAGOON GUARDS. In consequence of the regiment being placed upon a decreased rate of pay, compensation was given to the officers; to the colonel 150*l.* per year; to the lieutenant-colonel a gratuity of 575*l.*; to the major 525*l.*; captains, each, 475*l.*; captain-lieutenant and lieutenants, each, 350*l.*; and the cornets, each, 250*l.* Every private man had the option of his discharge, or a bounty of two guineas if he continued to serve.

Several alterations were made in the uniform of the regiment. The officers were directed to wear an epaulette on each shoulder. The flask-string was removed from the pouch belt, and the width of the belts reduced from four inches and a half to three inches; and the equipment was assimilated, in every particular, to that of the regiments of dragoons.

The establishment was fixed at one colonel and captain, one lieutenant-colonel and captain, one major and captain, three captains, six lieutenants, six cornets, one chaplain, one adjutant, one surgeon, six troop quarter-masters, six serjeants, twelve corporals, six trumpeters, one hundred and fourteen private men, and six dismounted men. The several alterations having been completed, the change of establishment took place on the 1st of April, 1788, and from this date the regiment has borne the title of FIFTH DRAGOON GUARDS; but the appellation of GREEN HORSE has never been entirely discontinued.

1789

1790

In the following year, the regiment lost its colonel, General the Honourable John Fitz-William, who was succeeded on the 27th of August, 1789, by Lieutenant-General John Douglas, from the Fourteenth Foot. Lieutenant-General Douglas died on the 10th of November, 1790, and was succeeded by Major-General Thomas Bland, from the Lieutenant-Colonelcy of the Seventh Dragoons.

1793

After passing a period of nearly eighty years in Ireland, the regiment, having previously had a considerable augmentation made to its numbers, was ordered to hold itself in readiness for foreign service. This event was occasioned by the revolution which had taken place in France, where a party of republicans had seized the reins of government, had imprisoned the royal family, and had brought their sovereign to the scaffold; a proceeding which disorganized the state of society in one of the most civilized parts of the world,—gave rise to the formation of a new dynasty,—removed the basis on which the sovereign power was established,—and involved the great European states in a succession of destructive wars for a period of more than twenty years. Great Britain joined the confederacy against the regicide government of France, and sent, in the spring of 1793, a body of troops to the Netherlands, under the command of His Royal Highness the Duke of York. At the close of the summer, reinforcements were sent to Flanders, and on the 18th and 19th of September, the FIFTH DRAGOON GUARDS embarked at Dublin for the same destination.

1794

After occupying winter quarters in Flanders, the regiment took the field under the orders of Lieutenant-Colonel the Honourable R. Taylor, and entered on a scene of action in a part of Europe where it had, nearly a century before, acquired numerous honours under the great MARLBOROUGH, and its conduct did not derogate from its ancient reputation. It was first employed in the attack of the enemy's post at *Prêmont*, on the 17th of April, 1794, but was not called upon to charge; and it subsequently formed part of the covering army during the siege of *Landrécies*.

While this siege was in progress, the British troops, under the Duke of York, were encamped at *Cateau*. On the morning of the 26th of April, which was gloomy and dark, and a thick mist covered the face of nature, the advance of an hostile force was heard, but its movements could not be discerned. At length, the rays of the sun revealed the movements of a

French force of thirty thousand men, under Lieutenant-General Chapuy; and a body of cavalry, of which the FIFTH DRAGOON GUARDS formed part, was detached, under Lieutenant-General Otto, against the enemy's left flank, while a sharp attack was made on the enemy's front. This movement was conducted with great caution, the enemy's flank was turned, the trumpets sounded a charge, and the British horsemen rushed with irresistible fury upon the ranks of the hostile legions. The French were overthrown and defeated; their commander, Lieutenant-General Chapuy, a number of officers and men, and thirty-five pieces of cannon were captured, and their flying divisions were pursued with immense slaughter to the gates of Cambray. The Duke of York passed the highest commendations on the FIFTH DRAGOON GUARDS and other troops detached against the enemy's left flank, and declared they had "*all acquired immortal honour to themselves.*" His Royal Highness further stated, "*the conduct of the British cavalry was beyond all praise.*" The loss of the regiment on this occasion was nine men and twenty-three horses killed; one officer, one quarter-master, eight men and nine horses, wounded; four men and twenty-three horses missing.

After the surrender of Landrécies, the British forces took up a position in front of *Tournay*, where they repulsed an attack of the enemy on the 10th of May. During the action, a favourable opportunity presented itself for attacking the enemy's right flank; Lieutenant-General Harcourt was detached with sixteen squadrons of British and two of Austrian cavalry, and attacked the enemy with so much resolution and intrepidity, that they immediately began their retreat, in the course of which they were soon broken, and they sustained great loss, including thirteen pieces of cannon, and above four hundred officers and men taken prisoners.

A combined attack was made on the French positions on the 17th of May, but failed from some of the columns not arriving in time at the posts allotted to them.

On the 22nd of May, the French attacked the British position in front of *Tournay* with an immense force. The FIFTH DRAGOON GUARDS were

formed up ready for action on their camp ground all the day; but the French did not attack that part of the line; and they were repulsed in their attempts in the other parts of the field.

At length, the defeat of the Austrians having rendered the position occupied by the British in front of Tournay no longer tenable, the troops were withdrawn, and the campaign degenerated into a series of retreats, which were ably conducted under numerous difficulties.

1795

During this short but eventful campaign the British troops had maintained their ancient reputation; but the army was not of sufficient numbers to cope with the enormous masses of the enemy, which darkened the land like a gloomy tempest. In the retreat through Holland, and in the distresses and privations of the winter campaign amidst snow and ice, the FIFTH DRAGOON GUARDS took part, and in the early part of 1795 they arrived in Germany.

The regiment remained in Germany during the following summer, and encamped in one of the plains of the Duchy of Bremen, under the orders of Major-General Sir David Dundas; and in November it embarked for England.

1796

In October, 1796, the regiment proceeded to Ireland, which country was in a state bordering on open rebellion. The malcontents had entered into arrangements with the republican government of France, and a French armament was prepared, under the orders of General Hoche, to assist the Irish Roman Catholics in effecting their separation from England, and in forming themselves into a republic. On the 24th of December the French fleet appeared in Bantry Bay; and the FIFTH DRAGOON GUARDS were despatched by forced marches to oppose the landing of the enemy. The French fleet was, however, partly dispersed by a storm, and the remainder returned to France without attempting to land.

1797

In 1797 the regiment was encamped, with several other corps, on the Curragh of Kildare, and was there reviewed by Lieutenant-General Sir David Dundas, who expressed, in orders, his approbation of its discipline and appearance. Its establishment at this period was seven hundred officers and men.

1798

The disaffection which had so long prevailed among the Roman Catholics in Ireland, had continued to acquire additional rancour and vehemence, and the passions of the misguided peasantry having been wrought, by wicked demagogues, into fury and madness, they neglected the affairs of civil life, provided themselves with arms, and broke out into open rebellion in the summer of 1798. The FIFTH DRAGOON GUARDS were on Dublin duty at the time, and were so distinguished for loyalty and steady conduct that the Lord-Lieutenant committed to the regiment the military charge of the capital.

One squadron under the command of Brevet Lieutenant-Colonel Sherlock was detached from Dublin into the counties of Wicklow and Wexford, and was engaged in the action at *Arklow* on the 9th of June, when thirty thousand insurgents, headed by their priests in clerical vestments, attacked the town with great fury, but were repulsed with the loss of an immense number of men. From the circumstance of there being no force of any consequence to prevent the rebels marching upon the capital, this was an action of the greatest importance, and was most obstinately contested.

The same squadron was afterwards instrumental in relieving the loyalists in the town of *Ballycarnen*, where they were besieged by the rebels, and had only a small party of militia to assist in the defence of the place. The cavalry advanced with great bravery, and was assailed by a sharp fire from behind the fences, and a barrier of carts and other vehicles formed across the road, which it was found impossible to force by cavalry alone, and the troops retired until a body of infantry arrived; when the whole advanced,—routed the rebels, and pursued them with great slaughter.

Lieutenant-Colonel Sherlock was afterwards engaged with the squadron of the FIFTH DRAGOON GUARDS under his orders, at *Gorey*, and charged the rebels several times with success.

The same squadron was also engaged in the action at *Vinegar Hill*,—the stronghold of the rebels, where the most inhuman tragedies had been committed on hundreds of Protestants. This post was attacked on the 21st of June, and the insurgents were routed with great slaughter and many prisoners were captured. The squadron of the FIFTH DRAGOON GUARDS charged and pursued the rebels, and took many prisoners. It afterwards overtook an insurgent corps near a place called *White Hills*, where, after a sharp contest, the rebels were routed, and they fled in all directions.

While these events were transpiring, another detachment of the regiment was employed in the county of Kildare, and had several skirmishes with bands of insurgents.

A patrole of the regiment, commanded by Captain Pack, proceeding towards *Prosperous*, encountered one hundred rebels well mounted and equipped; the Dragoon Guards instantly charged with signal valour and intrepidity, routed their adversaries at the first shock, killed twenty on the spot, and captured eight horses.

When the rebellion was nearly suppressed, the French endeavoured to revive the contest by sending General Humbert with about a thousand men, who landed at Killala on the 22d of August. The FIFTH DRAGOON GUARDS marched from Dublin to oppose the combined rebel and French forces, and were attached to the column under the Marquis of Cornwallis's command. The action at *Ballinamuck* on the 8th of September followed; the French surrendered themselves prisoners of war, and the insurgents were dispersed. After the action, the Marquis of Cornwallis selected a squadron of the FIFTH DRAGOON GUARDS, commanded by Captain (afterwards Sir William) Ponsonby, to escort him on his return to Dublin.

1799

The rebellion in Ireland having been suppressed, the FIFTH DRAGOON GUARDS were embarked in 1799, in order to join the expedition to Holland, commanded by His Royal Highness the Duke of York; but the order for their proceeding on this service was countermanded, and after disembarking at Liverpool, they marched into quarters in Herefordshire and Gloucestershire.

1802

1803

After the conclusion of the Treaty of Amiens, a reduction of two troops was made in the establishment; but on the breaking out of the war in 1803, the army was again augmented, and an addition of two troops was again made to the strength of the regiment.

1804

In the following year King George III. was pleased to confer upon the regiment the distinguished title of THE PRINCESS CHARLOTTE OF WALES'S REGIMENT OF DRAGOON GUARDS, in honour of Her Royal Highness the Princess Charlotte Carolina Augusta, daughter of George William Frederick Prince of Wales (afterwards George IV.), by Carolina Amelia Elizabeth, second daughter of the Duke of Brunswick Wolfenbuttel. The Princess Charlotte of Wales exhibited in her early life a most amiable disposition with excellent traits of character, and, being considered as the future sovereign of Great Britain, the nation saw in her qualities calculated to adorn the throne, and to make a great and civilized people happy; hence, the conferring of Her Royal Highness's title on the regiment, was considered a special mark of His Majesty's favour and approbation.

1805

1808

The regiment proceeded to Ireland in 1805, and remained in that country until the summer of 1808, when it returned to England.

1811

On the 8th of July, 1811, His Royal Highness the Prince of Wales, who was Regent of the United Kingdom during the indisposition of King

George III., reviewed the regiment on Wimbledon common, on which occasion it was commanded by its Colonel, the veteran General Thomas Bland, and the Prince Regent was graciously pleased to express his approbation of its appearance, and of the rapidity and brilliant execution of its movements; and as the regiment was about to proceed on foreign service, the most lively anticipations of its achievements at the theatre of war were produced. It was not, at this period, mounted on horses of so heavy a description as formerly; but, while it bore the title of a heavy cavalry regiment, and retained sufficient weight for a powerful charge in line, it had acquired a lightness which rendered it available for every description of service. The heavy cavalry corps which formerly constituted so important a portion of the armies of England, had been improved in efficiency and usefulness by mounting them on horses of a lighter description.

The occasion of the FIFTH DRAGOON GUARDS proceeding abroad at this period, was the attempt made by that tyrannical power which had risen out of the French revolution, of which Napoleon Bonaparte had become the head, to subjugate the kingdoms of Spain and Portugal: the inhabitants of those countries were in arms against the usurper; a British force commanded by Lord Wellington had been sent to their aid; and this regiment was one of the corps selected to reinforce the army under his lordship's command.

Six troops of this regiment, amounting to five hundred and forty-four officers and men, commanded by Lieutenant-Colonel the Honourable William Ponsonby, embarked at Portsmouth on the 12th of August, and having landed at Lisbon on the 4th of September, occupied quarters at Belem about six weeks, and afterwards advanced up the country. When the army went into quarters for the winter, the FIFTH DRAGOON GUARDS were stationed at Thomar.

1812

The army resumed operations in the beginning of January, 1812, with the siege and capture of Ciudad Rodrigo: and in March the FIFTH DRAGOON

GUARDS proceeded into the south of Spain to watch the movements of Marshal Soult, and to cover the siege of *Badajoz*. The regiment arrived, with the remainder of its brigade (the Third and Fourth Dragoons), at Borba, in the Alentejo, on the 5th of March, crossed the Guadiana on the 15th, and formed the van of the covering army until it arrived at the foot of an extensive chain of mountains called the Sierra Morena. On the advance of Marshal Soult, the covering army retired upon Albuhera. The fortress of *Badajoz* was captured by storm on the 6th of April; and in a few days afterwards the regiment had an opportunity of distinguishing itself in action with the enemy. A large body of cavalry advanced upon *Llerena*; the FIFTH DRAGOON GUARDS marched on the 10th of April to Los Santos, and continued their route during the night to Bienvenida,—proceeding a distance of sixty miles without halting, and the last four miles at a brisk pace, through a country abounding with obstructions; then forming with celerity, advanced through a grove of olive-trees, beyond which a body of French cavalry, of more than thrice the numbers of the regiment, was formed up. The sight of so numerous an enemy did not intimidate the FIFTH DRAGOON GUARDS; but acted as a spur to their energies, and excited them to exertions which evinced their native valour and intrepidity, and occasioned them to rival the deeds of their predecessors in the field of glory. The fatigues of the previous march were forgotten, and the gallant troopers charged with such spirit and resolution, that the French squadrons were broken, and being also attacked by the light brigade, they retired in disorder under cover of their infantry and artillery, leaving behind about one hundred killed and wounded, and one lieutenant-colonel, two captains, one lieutenant, and one hundred and forty men prisoners, also nearly one hundred horses. Actions in which the numbers engaged are not very great, do not produce, in their bearing on the affairs of nations, very important results, hence they are often overlooked, or but slightly noticed, by general historians; yet on these occasions individual corps often distinguish themselves in an eminent

degree; and the excellent conduct of the British cavalry at *Llerena*, elicited the following orders:—

"Lafra, 12th April, 1812.

"CAVALRY ORDERS.

"Lieutenant-General Sir Stapleton Cotton begs Major-General Le Marchant and the Honourable Lieutenant-Colonel Ponsonby will accept his best thanks, for the gallant and judicious manner in which they commanded their brigades yesterday, and he requests they will make known to the officers commanding regiments, the lieutenant-general's high approbation of their conduct, as well as of the zeal and attention displayed by all ranks. The order which was preserved by the troops in pursuing the enemy, and the quickness with which they formed after every attack, does infinite credit to the commanding officers, and is a convincing proof of the good discipline of the several regiments.

"The Lieutenant-General was very much satisfied with the conduct of the Third and Fourth Dragoons, in supporting the Fifth Dragoon Guards and Major-General Anson's brigade.

"To Lieutenant-Colonel Elley, Sir Stapleton's warmest thanks are due, for the great assistance he derived from the zeal and activity displayed by that officer; and the Lieutenant-General begs that Captain White and Captain Baron Deckan will accept his acknowledgments for the assistance they afforded him yesterday. Sir Stapleton Cotton has only to assure the cavalry that their gallant and regular conduct yesterday has made him, if possible, more proud than ever of the high command entrusted to him.

"STAPLETON COTTON,

"LIEUTENANT-GENERAL."

"OLIVENZA, 15TH APRIL, 1812.

"BRIGADE ORDERS.

"Major-General Le Marchant has great satisfaction in conveying to his brigade the approbation and thanks of Lieutenant-General Sir Stapleton Cotton commanding the cavalry, for their gallant conduct near Llerena on the 11th instant.

"Whilst the Major-General is perfectly satisfied with the zeal shown by every individual of the brigade in the execution of his duty on that occasion, he considers that *the charge made by the* FIFTH DRAGOON GUARDS *deserves his particular admiration and approval, and he requests that* MAJOR PRESCOTT *and the officers of that corps will accept his best thanks, as well for their services as for the credit which their gallant conduct reflects on the command which he has the honour to hold.*

"T. HUTCHINS,
"BRIGADE-MAJOR."

These orders were forwarded to the depôt of the regiment in England, to be inserted in the records, accompanied by a letter, of which the following is an extract:—

"*Crato, Portugal, 7th May, 1812.*

"SIR,—I have great pleasure in communicating to you, by direction of Colonel Ponsonby, the cavalry and brigade orders issued on a late occasion, when the FIFTH DRAGOON GUARDS attacked a very superior enemy, and forced him to retire with the loss of about one hundred killed and wounded, besides one lieutenant-colonel, two captains, one lieutenant, and one hundred and forty men taken prisoners, with near one hundred horses. This affair presents a pledge of the future good conduct of the regiment whenever an opportunity again appears of meeting the enemy, and must be peculiarly gratifying to you and to the remainder of the corps at the depôt in England, to hear from such undoubted authority, that the regiment still continues to support that high character which it gained on many former glorious occasions, and in our estimation this last is not the least:—the regiment having, previous to the attack on three times its numbers of the enemy's best cavalry, made a forced march of upwards of sixty miles without halting,—four of the last of which was at a very brisk pace, through a difficult country, over rocks, ravines, and stone walls; then forming with unexampled celerity, and charging with equal and regular rapidity through a grove of olive-trees until it came in contact with the enemy, who retired in great disorder under the cover of

his infantry and guns. Our loss in this brilliant affair was comparatively trifling, as will be seen by the subjoined statement of the names of the brave men who fell.

"W. JACKSON,

"ADJUTANT."

Thus the DRAGOON GUARDS of the nineteenth century are found rivalling the celebrated heavy HORSE of the preceding ages. The regiment lost, on this occasion, one corporal and fourteen private men killed; Major Prescot, Lieutenant Walker, three serjeants, one corporal, and twenty-one private men wounded.

A detachment of the FIFTH DRAGOON GUARDS escorted the prisoners captured on this occasion to the fortress of Elvas in Portugal. The regiment afterwards marched to Crato.

Advancing from Crato into Spain, the FIFTH DRAGOON GUARDS took part in the movements by which the French were driven from Salamanca, and the forts at that city were besieged and captured.

After the capture of the forts, the regiment advanced upon Toro, but was subsequently ordered to retire to Alaejos to support a body of troops, under Lieutenant-General Sir Stapleton Cotton, posted on the Trabancos; and several retrograde movements followed, which were succeeded by the battle of *Salamanca*. During the night before this eventful day, while the regiment was dismounted, a violent storm occurred. The thunder rolled with tremendous violence over the heads of the men and horses; the lightning played in sheets of fire and shed its blazing gleams upon the polished arms; and the rain fell in torrents. One flash fell among the FIFTH DRAGOON GUARDS; the terrified horses breaking loose galloped wildly about in the dark, and every additional clap of thunder and blaze of lightning augmented the confusion. Twenty men of the regiment were trampled down and disabled, and several horses escaped into the French lines.

On the morning of the memorable 22d of July, the FIFTH DRAGOON GUARDS, commanded by Colonel the Honourable William Ponsonby,

moved from their bivouac and formed in the rear of the centre of the position occupied by the allied army.

While the French commander was manœuvring, Lord Wellington took advantage of an injudicious movement, and ordered his divisions forward to attack their adversaries, when the FIFTH DRAGOON GUARDS took ground to their right, passed the village of Arapiles, and advancing in support of the third and fifth divisions, were exposed to a heavy cannonade. The French army, being attacked at the moment it was making a complicated evolution, was unable to withstand the British forces; in a short time, a favourable opportunity for a charge of the heavy cavalry occurred, and the FIFTH DRAGOON GUARDS, and Third and Fourth Dragoons, were ordered to attack.[10] The bugles sounded; the brigade moved forward, increasing its pace, with Major-General Le Marchant at its head, and a most animated scene presented itself. The din of battle was heard on every side; clouds of dust and rising columns of smoke darkened the air, and enveloped the foaming squadrons as they dashed forward and shook the ground with their trampling hoofs. In front, the glittering bayonets and waving colours of French infantry were dimly seen through the thickened atmosphere; these formidable ranks of war were, in an instant, broken and overthrown by the terrific charge of this brigade; the resolute troopers, mingling with their discomfited antagonists, cut them down with a dreadful carnage, while the British infantry raised shouts of triumph and applause at the success of the cavalry, and numbers of the enemy laid down their arms, and surrendered prisoners of war. Major-General Le Marchant was shot through the body, which terminated the career of that gallant and talented officer; the command of the brigade devolved on the brave Colonel the Honourable William Ponsonby of the FIFTH DRAGOON GUARDS, and the officers and men of the regiment, emulating the heroic fire and energy of their favourite leader, performed deeds of valour worthy the high character of their corps. Having subdued one body of infantry, they continued their career through a wood in their front without waiting to re-form their

ranks; another formidable mass of fresh adversaries presented itself; the undaunted heavy horsemen, conscious of their power, flushed with success, stimulated to new energies by seeing Lieutenant-General Sir Stapleton Cotton and his staff at their head, rushed forward with reckless fury; though assailed by a volley of musketry, which proved fatal to many, the survivors passed through the curling smoke, scarcely seeming to touch the ground, and the next moment the French column was broken with a dreadful crash. That mass of infantry, a moment before so menacing and conspicuous, was become a confused rabble, while the victorious troopers, exulting in uncontrollable might, trampled down and plunged their horses through the enemy's ranks, sabring their dismayed adversaries, and producing havoc and confusion on every hand.[11] Five guns and more than two thousand prisoners were captured, and a division of French infantry was destroyed; two guns were seized by the FIFTH DRAGOON GUARDS, and sent to the rear immediately after they broke through the enemy's ranks. Such were the splendid results of this gallant and dreadful charge, in which the weight, prowess, and daring impetuosity of the FIFTH DRAGOON GUARDS, and Third and Fourth Dragoons, seconded by the light brigade, proved irresistible, and contributed materially in deciding the fortune of a battle in which the French army sustained a decisive overthrow, and eleven guns and two *eagles* remained in possession of the conquerors. The British commander stated in his public despatch,—"The cavalry, under Sir Stapleton Cotton, made a most gallant and successful charge upon a body of French infantry, which they overthrew and cut to pieces:" Colonel the Honourable William Ponsonby was presented with a gold medal for his conduct as commanding officer; and the regiment was afterwards rewarded with the honour of bearing the word SALAMANCA on its standards and appointments. Its loss was Captain Osborne, two serjeants, one corporal, and twelve private men killed; Lieutenant Christie, one serjeant, one corporal, and fourteen private men wounded.

FIFTH (THE PRINCESS CHARLOTTE OF WALES'S) REGIMENT OF DRAGOON GUARDS,

At the Battle of Salamanca, 22nd July, 1812.

[*To face page 60.*

The left squadron of the FIFTH DRAGOON GUARDS was attached to Major-General Bock's brigade of heavy German cavalry, and sent in pursuit of the wreck of the French army, which retreated by Alba upon Valladolid; the French rear-guard was overtaken about three leagues beyond *Alba de Tormes*, a sharp engagement ensued, and about nine hundred prisoners were captured.

Colonel the Honourable William Ponsonby, of the Fifth Dragoon Guards, having been appointed to the staff of the army, and to the command of the heavy cavalry brigade, issued the following order on the subject:—

"*Camp near Flores de Avila,*
25th July, 1812.

"REGIMENTAL ORDERS,

"His Excellency, the commander of the forces, having been pleased to appoint Colonel Ponsonby to the staff of this army, and to the distinguished honour of commanding this brigade, Major Prescott will be pleased to take upon himself the command of the regiment.

"The FIFTH DRAGOON GUARDS well know how highly Colonel Ponsonby has always prized the honour of commanding them; and if the pride he has long felt in the command of a regiment deservedly of such high character admitted of augmentation, its most gallant and glorious achievements in the field, as well as its soldier-like conduct in quarters, since its arrival in this country, could not fail to enhance it. He assures the officers and men of the regiment, that it is now with considerable regret he takes his leave of them as their regimental commanding officer, although in the course of professional promotion; and he requests Major Prescott, the officers, non-commissioned officers, and the whole of the regiment, will accept his warm and sincere thanks for the past, as well as his heartfelt and anxious good wishes for the future. May the Fifth Dragoon Guards long continue to be ranked as second to none in His Majesty's service."

The regiment accompanied the army in the subsequent movements, and in the advance upon the capital of Spain; and it formed part of the personal escort of the Marquis of Wellington when he entered Madrid on the 12th of August; it was formed up at the Segovia-gate, when his lordship received the keys from the municipality. The FIFTH DRAGOON GUARDS entered the city amidst the acclamations of the inhabitants, and occupied quarters there until the 18th of August.

Leaving the metropolis of Spain to engage in operations against the French army, the regiment proceeded to St. Ildefonso, remained there a few days, and afterwards proceeded to the vicinity of *Burgos*, where the enemy was found in position on the 17th of September. The FIFTH DRAGOON GUARDS, and Third and Fourth Dragoons, were ordered to the front, and dispositions were made for the attack; but the French

commander withdrew his forces, leaving a strong garrison in the castle of Burgos. This fortress was besieged, and the regiment, forming part of the covering army, was stationed at Villamar, the head quarters of the cavalry. On the 19th of October, the enemy attempted to relieve the besieged, and attacked and carried the village of Quintanapalla; the left wing of infantry and FIFTH DRAGOON GUARDS, and Third and Fourth Dragoons, advanced to retake the village, but on the approach of this force the French retreated.

At length, the movements of the superior numbers of the enemy, rendered it necessary for the main army to unite with the forces under Lieutenant-General Sir Rowland Hill, and a retreat was resolved upon. Withdrawing from Burgos with great secrecy on the night of the 21st of October, the army commenced its celebrated retreat to the frontiers of Portugal, which was performed under peculiar difficulties, and in presence of an immense superiority of numbers, with the same signal ability which distinguished all the operations of the British commander, who evinced, on many occasions during this war, the sublimity of military talent.

On the 23rd of October, the army continued its retreat in two columns; the FIFTH DRAGOON GUARDS, and Third and Fourth Dragoons, covering the retreat of the column from Hormillos; the enemy menaced the rear with an immense force of cavalry, but was unable to make a serious impression, and the British troops bivouacked that night on the hills above Cordovilla. Resuming the march an hour before daylight on the following morning, the column passed the bridge of Cordovilla and crossed the Carrion, covered by Colonel Ponsonby's brigade, and the head quarters were established at Duenas, from whence two squadrons of the FIFTH DRAGOON GUARDS and Third Dragoons were detached, to cover the working parties employed in mining the bridges of Palencia for destruction; but the French advancing in great force gained possession of the bridges in an unbroken state. On the 26th the army resumed its retrograde movement, crossed the Pisuerga at Cabeçon, and occupied that town and its vicinity until the 29th, when it again retired, and, having

crossed the Douro, occupied a position beyond that river several days. On the 6th of November the army retreated on Salamanca; on the 15th it resumed its march, and having crossed the Agueda, proceeded into quarters in Portugal. The FIFTH DRAGOON GUARDS halted eight days at Gallegos, in the province of Biera, and afterwards proceeded to Ervidal, where they remained until the 28th of December, and subsequently marched to Goes.

Thus ended this eventful campaign, in which the allied army, after capturing the two important fortresses of Ciudad Rodrigo and Badajoz, gaining the glorious victory of Salamanca, and penetrating to the metropolis of Spain, was forced, by the superior number of the enemy's concentrated forces, to return to its former posts. The gigantic power to which the French revolution had given birth was, however, on the eve of being broken; Bonaparte, the tyrant of Europe, had resolved on the fatal expedition to Russia, where he lost a powerful army in the snow, and the victory at Salamanca was the precursor of greater triumphs over the disturbers of christendom. The immense distance marched by the FIFTH DRAGOON GUARDS during the year 1812, with the scarcity of forage and constant exposure to every description of weather, occasioned the loss of many horses; it has been computed that the regiment marched about two thousand miles within twelve months.

1813

The regiment was again in motion in February, 1813, and having taken post at Viride, in the valley of the Mondego, occupied that station until the middle of April, when it proceeded to Guimarers, and halted there seventeen days.

In May the army commenced operations with a prospect of more splendid results than on any former occasion; and Colonel Ponsonby's brigade, which still consisted of the FIFTH DRAGOON GUARDS, and Third and Fourth Dragoons, traversed the wild and mountainous country of Trasos-Montes, and crossed the Esla on the 26th of May. The enemy, no longer possessing that superiority of numbers by which he had formerly

gained so many advantages, abandoned the line of the Douro; Ponsonby's brigade directed its march on Valencia, passed that town, and advanced on Burgos. On the 12th of June, the brigade overtook the enemy's rear-guard on the heights of Estepar, when the Third Dragoons were detached to cut off part of the enemy's force, in which they succeeded, and Captain Miles, of the Fourteenth Dragoons, charging, took some prisoners and one gun. During the succeeding night, the French blew up the castle of Burgos, and retired behind the Ebro. Colonel Ponsonby's brigade moved to the left, and after traversing a romantic tract of country, over mountains and rugged precipices, crossed the Ebro on the 15th of June, and advanced on *Vittoria*, where the enemy concentrated his forces and took up a defensive position.

At day-break, on the morning of the 21st of June, the allied army advanced against the enemy, and the FIFTH DRAGOON GUARDS supported the columns of attack. The British infantry dislodged their adversaries from the several eminences and strong posts at the point of the bayonet, and being supported and sustained by the cavalry, forced the enemy, after a dreadful slaughter had taken place, to retreat with the loss of his guns, ammunition, and baggage. The cavalry, having been prevented by the nature of the ground from charging during the early part of the day, was enabled to dash forward towards the close of the action, and to complete the rout and discomfiture of the French army. The FIFTH DRAGOON GUARDS had only one man wounded on this occasion. Their gallant bearing throughout the day, procured them the honour of displaying the word VITTORIA on their standards and appointments, and their commanding officer, Lieutenant-Colonel Prescott, was rewarded with a gold medal. The brigade continued the pursuit of the enemy on the following day, and on the 27th of June was detached, to endeavour to intercept the retreat of a division of the French army, under General Clausel; but this body of troops escaped to France by the pass of Jaca. The FIFTH DRAGOON GUARDS had advanced to Tafalla, where they remained fourteen days, when, forage becoming scarce, they proceeded to

Miranda. In the mean time, the infantry having blockaded Pampeluna, penetrated the Pyrenean mountains. Marshal Soult advanced to relieve Pampeluna, when these celebrated mountains became the scene of several fierce and deadly contests between the English and French infantry, and the cavalry were ordered forward in support. The FIFTH DRAGOON GUARDS left Mirando on the 26th of July, and were formed up at the foot of the Pyrenees during the actions in the mountains towards the end of the month, when the French were defeated and forced to retire with great loss.

The heavy cavalry not being required in the mountain operations of the army, the FIFTH DRAGOON GUARDS marched to Estella, a city of Navarre, where they arrived on the 11th of August, and remained until the 27th of December, when, forage becoming scarce, they proceeded to the plains of Vittoria, and occupied Guérena and adjacent villages.

1814

Towards the end of February, 1814, the FIFTH DRAGOON GUARDS again advanced. After passing through the Pyrenean mountains, they entered France, and followed the route of the French troops retreating on Bayonne. On the 19th of March, the army, under Marshal Soult, was discovered in position near *Tarbes*, when a division of infantry and Major-General Ponsonby's brigade of cavalry were ordered to turn the enemy's right flank at Rabastens, but the French, being thus threatened, retired. Following the rear of the French army, the brigade crossed the Garonne, on a pontoon bridge, at St. Roques, on the 31st of March, and seized the bridge on the Arriege, at Cintagabelle; but the roads were found so bad in this direction, that the troops were recalled, and the pontoon bridge being removed to Grenade, the brigade passed the river on the 4th of April, took post at Grissolles, and placed a strong picquet on the road to Montauban.

In the mean time, the French army had taken up a strong position to cover *Toulouse*, where they were attacked by the allied army on the 10th of April. The infantry attacked the enemy's entrenchments with their usual

intrepidity. The cavalry brigade, consisting of the FIFTH DRAGOON GUARDS, and Third and Fourth Dragoons, was commanded on this occasion by Lieutenant-Colonel Lord Charles Manners; it was employed in supporting the Spanish forces, and, by its firm countenance, it enabled them, after having been thrown into some confusion, to rally and re-form their broken ranks. It also saved the Portuguese guns from being captured by the French, and subsequently supported Lieutenant-General Clinton's division: at length, the enemy was driven from his works, and forced to take shelter in the town. The FIFTH DRAGOON GUARDS had one corporal killed and Cornet Lucas wounded; and their services on this occasion were rewarded with the honour of bearing the word TOULOUSE on their standards and appointments.

Shortly after this victory hostilities were terminated, by the removal of Buonaparte from the throne of France, and the restoration of the Bourbon dynasty. Thus ended the toils and conflicts of this destructive war, and the FIFTH DRAGOON GUARDS, after traversing kingdoms, enduring privations, and gaining victories, had the gratification of witnessing the restoration of peace. The French forces, after fighting to add province to province, and kingdom to kingdom, to found new empires upon the ruins of conquered states, to subject mankind to the tyranny of a lawless despot, saw their hopes blasted, their conquests wrested from them, their country invaded and subject to the power of foreigners; but the British army, which fought under the immortal Wellington for the good of Europe,—for the welfare of other nations, preserved its own country from the horrors of war, and had the glory of conquering to establish the peace of Christendom.

The FIFTH DRAGOON GUARDS remained in cantonments until the 1st of June, when, having sent their dismounted men and heavy baggage to Bourdeaux, they commenced their march for Boulogne.[12] This long march, from one extremity of France to another, was performed in the short period of six weeks; and, previous to embarking, Major-General Ponsonby expressed to the three regiments in brigade orders, "the high

sense he entertained of their uniformly excellent conduct both in quarters and in the field:" adding, "It is a gratifying circumstance that, during the whole period of service, they have, in no instance, individually or collectively, incurred animadversion in general orders; that no individual of the brigade has been brought before a general court martial; and that not one instance has occurred (to the major-general's knowledge) of interior disagreement in the brigade. With equal truth the major-general can assert, that upon every occasion which has presented itself of acting against the enemy, whether regimentally or in brigade, they have nobly sustained the superiority of the British cavalry, and fully justified the high opinion so repeatedly expressed with regard to them by his Grace the Duke of Wellington. The three regiments will ever have to congratulate themselves on its having fallen to their lot to be the brigade employed in that glorious and effectual charge, which contributed in so eminent a degree to decide the fate of the day at SALAMANCA, and to secure the signal and complete defeat of the French army. It only remains for the major-general to declare his satisfaction at the exemplary conduct of the brigade during the march through France; and he concludes by requesting that Lieutenant-Colonel Lord Charles Manners, Lieutenant-Colonel Prescott, and Major Hugonin, will themselves accept, and have the goodness to communicate to the regiments under their respective commands, his best and warmest thanks for their zealous and steady services during the time he has had the honour of commanding the brigade, together with his earnest and sincere good wishes for their future welfare. He also requests Brigade-Major Hill will accept his best thanks for the zeal and assiduous attention with which he has discharged the duties of his situation."

The FIFTH DRAGOON GUARDS embarked at Boulogne on the 17th and 18th of July, landed at Dover on the 19th and 20th, and marched from thence to Woodbridge barracks, where the depôt and heavy baggage joined from Canterbury, and a reduction of two troops was made in the

establishment. In October the regiment marched to Ipswich and adjacents.

1815

In April, 1815, "His Royal Highness the Prince Regent was pleased, in the name and on the behalf of His Majesty, to approve of the FIFTH, OR PRINCESS CHARLOTTE OF WALES'S REGIMENT OF DRAGOON GUARDS, being permitted to bear on its standards and appointments (in addition to any other badges or devices which may have been heretofore granted to the regiment), the word 'PENINSULA,' in commemoration of its services during the late war in Portugal, Spain, and France, under the command of Field-Marshal the Duke of Wellington."

On the 8th of April, the regiment marched to Nottingham, Coventry, Northampton, and Leicester; and the return of Napoleon Buonaparte to France, in breach of the treaty of 1814, having occasioned a declaration of war, six troops were ordered to be held in readiness for foreign service; but, to the great regret of the officers and men, who panted for another opportunity of signalizing themselves under the Duke of Wellington, the order was subsequently countermanded in consequence of the number of young and untrained horses in the regiment.

In June, the officers and men of the FIFTH DRAGOON GUARDS received the painful intelligence of the fall of Major-General Sir William Ponsonby, G.C.B., at the battle of Waterloo.[13]

In July, the regiment marched to York, Sheffield, Leeds, Huddersfield, and Newcastle-upon-Tyne: in September, the several troops proceeded to Newcastle, in consequence of the riotous conduct of the seamen in the ports of that neighbourhood.

1816

In January, 1816, the regiment occupied Newcastle, York, Carlisle, Penrith, and Whitehaven; during the summer, it proceeded to Ireland, and, arriving at Dublin towards the end of August, remained on duty in that garrison six months.

General Bland died at Isleworth on the 14th of October, 1816; and on the 18th of that month, His Royal Highness Prince Leopold of Saxe-Coburg of Saalfield, K.G., G.C.B., G.C.H., was appointed Colonel of the FIFTH, OR PRINCESS CHARLOTTE OF WALES'S REGIMENT OF DRAGOON GUARDS.

1817

The regiment left Ireland in February, 1817, and proceeded to Scotland, where it remained until the autumn; and, on its arrival in England, it occupied Ipswich, Norwich, &c.

THE PRINCESS CHARLOTTE OF WALES died on the 6th of November of this year, but the title of the regiment is continued, in honour of the memory of that amiable Princess.

1818

1819

1820

In July, 1818, the regiment proceeded to York, where the establishment was reduced to fifty men and thirty-four horses per troop; in the summer of 1819, it marched to Birmingham, Coventry, and Wolverhampton; in April, 1820, to Manchester,[14] Oldham, and Ashton; and in August of the same year, to York, Leeds, and Huddersfield.

On the 3rd of September a communication was received from Major-General Sir John Byng commanding the northern district, enclosing a letter from the Military Secretary, wherein it was stated that "His Royal Highness the commander-in-chief approved highly of the general good conduct, loyalty, and steadiness of the regiment, of which favourable report was made to His Royal Highness from all quarters."

1821

In April, 1821, the FIFTH DRAGOON GUARDS marched to Scotland, and occupied Hamilton, Glasgow, and Paisley: in August the regiment proceeded to Ireland, and was quartered at Belfast, Belturbet, Sligo, Enniskillen, and Dundalk; at the same time a reduction of two troops was

made in the establishment, leaving the numbers six troops, of three officers, fifty-five men, and forty-two troop-horses each.

1822

1823

1824

The regiment marched to Porto Bello barracks, Dublin, in July, 1822; from thence to Ballinrobe, Gort, Loughrea, Athlone, Roscommon, and Dunmore, in May, 1823: and in July, 1824, to Dundalk and Belturbet.

1825

The regiment left Ireland in April, 1825, and proceeding to Scotland, was stationed at Glasgow and Hamilton.

1826

Leaving Scotland in the spring of 1826, the regiment proceeded to York and Newcastle-upon-Tyne, with a detachment on revenue duty at Beverley. In April the regiment was ordered into the manufacturing districts of Yorkshire, in consequence of some disturbance amongst the operatives, but returned to York in June.

1827

In February, 1827, the regiment proceeded to Leeds, Rochdale, and Sheffield.

1828

1829

In May, 1828, the regiment marched to Dorchester, Weymouth, Troubridge, and Christ Church, with detached parties on coast duty, and in the following summer it proceeded to Canterbury.

1830

Leaving Canterbury in April, 1830, the regiment marched to Coventry and Birmingham. In July of the same year His Majesty, King William IV., was pleased to command that the FIFTH DRAGOON GUARDS should proceed to Windsor, to undertake the duties usually performed by the household cavalry; and, shortly after their arrival there, they were inspected by Field Marshal Prince Leopold of Saxe-Coburg, when his Royal Highness

expressed himself much gratified with the excellent appearance and discipline of his corps.

On the 14th of August the FIFTH DRAGOON GUARDS, commanded by Prince Leopold in person, were reviewed in the barrack square at Windsor, by his Majesty King William IV., accompanied by the Queen and other members of the royal family. His Majesty having made a minute inspection of the regiment, was pleased to express his high approbation of its martial appearance and efficiency: and the officers were then severally presented to the King, by Prince Leopold. After the review their Majesties, with the other members of the royal family and distinguished personages present, partook of a *déjeuné* prepared by order of Prince Leopold, under tents on the green, and in the officers' mess-room.

His Majesty, accompanied by Lord Hill (the general commanding-in-chief) inspected the FIFTH DRAGOON GUARDS in the great quadrangle at Windsor Castle, on the 29th of August, and again expressed his royal approbation of their appearance and discipline.

In October of the same year the regiment marched to Maidstone and adjacent places. In the following month the head quarters proceeded to Tunbridge Wells, and, in consequence of the riotous conduct of the agricultural labourers in Sussex, the remainder of the corps was dispersed in various parts of that county. In December the head quarters proceeded to Brighton, and occupied the cavalry barrack at that town during His Majesty's residence at the Royal Pavilion.

1831

Prince Leopold of Saxe-Coburg having been elected king of the Belgians, resigned the commission of Colonel of the FIFTH DRAGOON GUARDS, and King William IV. was graciously pleased to confer that appointment on Lieutenant-General Sir John Slade, Bart. G.C.H., by commission, dated 20th July, 1831.

1834

The regiment embarked at Bristol on the 17th April, 1831, and landed at Dublin on the following day. It continued on duty at various stations in

Ireland until April, 1834, when it again returned to England, disembarked at Liverpool on the 22d of that month, and was stationed for one year at Manchester.

1835
1836
1837
1838

In May, 1835, the regiment proceeded to Scotland, from whence it returned in the following year, and was stationed at Leeds; in April, 1837, its head-quarters were established at Birmingham; and in May, 1838, at York.

The foregoing pages contain an account of the services of the FIFTH DRAGOON GUARDS to the termination of the year 1838, and its record bears ample testimony to the zeal and bravery which have been evinced by this distinguished corps on occasions when it has had an opportunity to attest its valour in presence of a foreign enemy.

Its noble and gallant conduct, as a regiment of HORSE, at the battle of the *Boyne* in 1690;—at the heights of *Schellenberg*;—also at the memorable battle of *Blenheim*, where the French and Bavarian armies were nearly destroyed, and their commander, standards, and colours were captured, in 1704;—its heroic achievements in 1705 at the forcing of the French lines at *Helixem* and *Neer-Hespen*, where it captured the standards of the Bavarian horse-guards;—the glorious part it took in annihilating one of the finest and best appointed armies France ever brought into the field, at *Ramilies* in 1706;—its intrepid bearing, as a corps of CUIRASSIERS, in 1708 in the field at *Oudenarde*, and in the action at *Wynendale*;—the valour it displayed in close combat with the French household troops at the sanguinary battle of *Malplaquet* in 1709;—the ardour it evinced in the movements and skirmishes which led to the capture of the fortress of *Bouchain* in 1711;—its gallantry as a corps of DRAGOON GUARDS in 1794 at the battle of *Cateau*, where the French commander, many officers and men, and thirty-five pieces of cannon were captured;—its brilliant charge

at *Llerena*;—its victorious career on the plains of *Salamanca* in 1812;—its spirited conduct at Vittoria in 1813;—and at Toulouse in 1814;—the eminent qualities it displayed on these and other occasions, as set forth in the public despatches and national records, afford most honourable proof that the FIFTH REGIMENT OF DRAGOON GUARDS has never lost sight of the ancient motto on its standards *Vestigia nulla retrorsum*.

The conduct of the regiment on home, as well as on foreign service, has, on all occasions, been such as to evince its usefulness, efficiency, and constant readiness to support the honour and dignity of the crown, and the prosperity of the country; thus holding forth a bright example to stimulate to good conduct the soldiers of the present and future ages, under all the circumstances of service in which the calls of their sovereign and country may occasion them to be placed.

FOOTNOTES:

[7] Charles Butler, second son of Thomas Earl of Ossory, and grandson of James first Duke of Ormond, was created Earl of the islands of Arran, in the county of Galway, in January, 1694. The Earl of Arran, mentioned at page 7, was the eldest son of William Duke of Hamilton, and obtained his father's title in 1698.

[8] This officer's name is spelt Napper, instead of Napier, in the lists of killed and wounded published at the time; but he is the same officer who was appointed Colonel of the regiment by King George I., on the 27th of May, 1717.

[9] "The Sunday following was appointed for a day of thanks-giving, and after divine service the army drew out to fire a *feu-de-joie* for the victory. Marshal Tallard and the officers with him were invited to ride out to see the army fire, which they did with much persuasion. Our generals paid Tallard the compliment of riding next the army, and ordered all the officers to salute him. When the firing was over, the Duke of Marlborough asked Tallard how he liked the army; he answered with a shrug, *Very well; but they have had the honour of beating the best troops in the world.* The Duke replied, *What will the world think of the troops that beat them?*"— *Parker's Memoirs.*

[10] The following very spirited description of the charge of the Fifth Dragoon Guards, and Third and Fourth Dragoons, is copied from Colonel Napier's admirable History of the Peninsular War:—

"While Pakenham, bearing onward with a conquering violence, was closing on their flank, and the fifth division advancing with a storm of fire on their front, the interval between the two attacks was suddenly filled with a whirling cloud of dust, which moving swiftly forward carried within its womb the trampling sound of a charging multitude. As it passed the left of the third division Le Marchant's heavy horsemen, flanked by Anson's light cavalry, broke forth from it at full speed, and the next instant twelve hundred French infantry though formed in several lines were trampled down with a terrible clamour and disturbance. Bewildered

75

and blinded, they cast away their arms and ran through the openings of the British squadrons stooping and demanding quarter, while the dragoons, big men and on big horses, rode onward smiting with their long glittering swords in uncontrollable power, and the third division followed at speed, shouting as the French masses fell in succession before this dreadful charge."

"Nor were these valiant swordsmen yet exhausted. Their own general, Le Marchant, and many officers had fallen, but Cotton and all his staff were at their head, and with ranks confused, and blended together in one mass, still galloping forward they sustained from a fresh column an irregular stream of fire which emptied a hundred saddles; yet with fine courage, and downright force, the survivors broke through this the third and strongest body of men that had encountered them, and Lord Edward Somerset, continuing his course at the head of one squadron, with a happy perseverance, captured five guns. The French left was entirely broken, more than two thousand prisoners were taken, the French light horsemen abandoned that part of the field, and Thomiere's division no longer existed as a military body. Anson's cavalry, which had passed quite over the hill, and had suffered little in the charge, was now joined by D'Urban's troopers, and took the place of Le Marchant's exhausted men; the heavy German dragoons followed in reserve, and with the third and fifth divisions and the guns formed one formidable line two miles in advance of where Pakenham first attacked, and that impetuous officer with unmitigated strength still pressed forward spreading terror and disorder on the enemy's left."

[11] The sixty-sixth French regiment of infantry of the line, was one of the corps which was nearly annihilated, and the staff of the drum-major of that regiment is preserved as a trophy by the FIFTH DRAGOON GUARDS, and carried on parades, &c., by the trumpet-major.

[12] While at Boulogne the regiment was inspected by Major-General Sir Henry Fane, who expressed much gratification at its condition after so long a march, and selected a number of horses to be given up to the

French government, for the purpose of mounting the royal guard of Louis XVIII.

[13] The Honourable William Ponsonby, (son of Lord Ponsonby,) after holding the commissions of ensign in Captain Bulwer's independent company, lieutenant in Captain Davis's independent company, and captain in the eighty-third regiment, was appointed major in the Loyal Irish Fencibles, in December, 1794: in March, 1798 he was removed to the majority of the Fifth Dragoon Guards, and he served with his regiment in Ireland during the rebellion, which broke out in the following summer. On the 1st of January, 1800, he was promoted to the rank of lieutenant-colonel in the army; in February, 1803, he was appointed lieutenant-colonel, in the Fifth Dragoon Guards; and on the 25th of July, 1810, he was advanced to the brevet rank of colonel. He commanded the six troops of the Fifth Dragoon Guards on foreign service in 1811, and 1812, and while at the theatre of war he was so conspicuous for a gallant and chivalrous spirit, with cheerful alacrity in moments of peril and privation, united with a kind and benevolent disposition, that he won the affection and esteem of those individuals who had the happiness of becoming acquainted with him, and he was the favourite of the troopers of his regiment. At the battle of Salamanca he led the Fifth Dragoon Guards to the charge with his characteristic zeal and gallantry; after the fall of Major-General Le Marchant he was appointed to the command of the heavy brigade, which he held until the end of the war; and no officer better qualified for that important trust, or one who possessed the confidence of the officers and men in a greater degree, could have been found in the army. He was promoted to the rank of major-general on the 4th of June, 1813; and was afterwards chosen a knight commander of the honourable military order of the Bath. On the recommencement of hostilities in 1815, this distinguished officer was placed on the staff of the army in Belgium, and appointed to the command of the second cavalry brigade, consisting of the Royal, Scots Greys, and Inniskilling dragoons, which corps he led to the charge of the French infantry at the battle of

Waterloo with that intrepidity for which he had always been so eminently distinguished. Having cut through the first column, he continued his career against fresh adversaries; while passing through a newly-ploughed field, which was so soft and miry from recent heavy rain that his charger sunk deeply in the soil at every step and became exhausted, he was attacked by a regiment of Polish lancers; being in front of his brigade, no one was near him except one aide-de-camp, and at the moment when his horse was unable to extricate itself, a body of lancers approached him at full speed. His own death he knew was inevitable; but supposing his aide-de-camp might escape, he drew from his bosom the picture of his lady, and was in the act of delivering it and his watch to his attendant, to be conveyed to his wife and family, when the lancers came up, and they were both speared on the spot. Thus fell the brave, the ingenuous Ponsonby, whose death occasioned deep sorrow in the Fifth Dragoon Guards, and the troopers expressed regret that they were not at Waterloo to revenge the death of their former commander, who had led them to battle and to victory. His death is thus alluded to by the Duke of Wellington in his public despatch. "I have received a report that Major-General Sir William Ponsonby is killed; and in announcing this intelligence I have to add the expression of my grief for the fate of an officer who had already rendered very brilliant and important services, and was an ornament to his profession."

[14]

Manchester, August 23d, 1820.

Sir,

Although the Fifth Dragoon Guards were only placed at Manchester as a temporary quarter, I should be wanting in what is due from me to that distinguished corps, did I withhold from you the expression of my admiration of it as a regiment, or from the officers, non-commissioned officers, and privates, my unqualified approbation of their conduct, and my satisfaction at the readiness and good-will with which they performed all the duties required of them whilst under my orders. I request you will

do me the honour to make known these my sentiments to them, with the assurance that it will be ever gratifying to me to hear of their continued welfare and prosperity.

I have &c.

JAMES LYON, Major-General.

Major Irwin, commanding Fifth Dragoon Guards.

SUCCESSION OF COLONELS

OF THE
FIFTH, OR PRINCESS CHARLOTTE OF WALES'S
REGIMENT OF DRAGOON GUARDS.

CHARLES EARL OF SHREWSBURY,

Appointed 29th of July, 1685.

CHARLES TALBOT succeeded, when in the seventh year of his age, to the title of EARL OF SHREWSBURY, on the decease of his father who died on the 16th of March, 1667, of a wound received in a duel with the Duke of Buckingham. In 1681 he was appointed lord-lieutenant of the county of Stafford; and having previously devoted much time to the consideration of the doctrines of Christianity, on the discovery of the Popish plot he abjured the tenets of the church of Rome. He, however, continued steadfast in his loyalty even to a Popish sovereign, and on the breaking out of the rebellion of the Duke of Monmouth in June, 1685, he raised a troop of horse for the service of King James II, and in the following month he was appointed colonel of the regiment which now bears the title of FIFTH DRAGOON GUARDS. He soon afterwards discovered that the arbitrary measures of the court were directed to the subversion of the Protestant religion, of which he was become a determined supporter; and having resigned his commission and mortgaged his estate for forty thousand pounds, he proceeded to Holland and made an offer of his sword and purse to the Prince of Orange, provided His Highness would attempt to deliver England from the power of the papists. From this period, until the revolution in 1688, his active mind was engaged in the glorious and patriotic labour of devising plans for the good of his native country, and he was one of the nobles in whom the Prince of Orange placed the greatest confidence, and by whose advice he was principally guided.

When William and Mary were elevated to the throne, the Earl of Shrewsbury was sworn of the Privy Council, and appointed principal Secretary of State; and in April, 1694, he was elected a Knight of the Most

Noble Order of the Garter, and created Marquis of Alton and DUKE OF SHREWSBURY. After devoting himself to the service of his king and country in the important office of principal Secretary of State, for a period of ten years, he sustained a serious injury in the breast, from an unlucky fall of his horse while hunting, which rendered him incapable of attending so closely to business as his office required, and he resigned the seals as Secretary of State, but was shortly afterwards appointed Lord Chamberlain of the Household. This office he resigned in 1700, in order to proceed to a warmer climate, and he resided for a short period at Montpellier in France. After the decease of the King of Spain and the accession of the Duke of Anjou to the throne of that kingdom, he quitted France and proceeded to Geneva, and subsequently crossed the Alps into Italy. After his return to England he was reappointed by Queen Anne to the office of Lord Chamberlain, and in 1712 he was appointed ambassador to the French court to finish the negociations for peace. In 1713 he was appointed Lord Lieutenant of Ireland; and in the reign of George I. he was a member of the Privy Council and Lord Chamberlain of the Household. He was one of the most accomplished gentlemen of the age in which he lived; was remarkably handsome in person, had an admirable address, was just in his dealings, and distinguished for gallantry among the ladies; but was studious and reserved as a public character. He died at Isleworth on the 1st of February, 1718.

MARMADUKE LORD LANGDALE,

Appointed 22d January, 1687.

This nobleman was the son of Sir Marmaduke Langdale of Holme, in Spaldingmore, Yorkshire, who, when the rebellion broke out in the reign of Charles I., raised at his own charge three companies of foot and a troop of horse for the king's service, with which force he defeated a party of Scots at Corbridge in Northumberland. Having been appointed to the command of a body of troops sent by the King from Oxford into Lincolnshire, he defeated Colonel Rosseter; then marching against Fairfax, put him to flight and relieved Pontefract Castle. He subsequently took

Berwick-upon-Tweed, and the castle of Carlisle, but being involved in the defeat of the Duke of Hamilton, he was taken prisoner at Preston. Having escaped from confinement he fled to the continent, and in February, 1658, he was elevated to the peerage by the title of BARON LANGDALE of Holme, in Spaldingmore, Yorkshire.

MARMADUKE, second LORD LANGDALE, imbibed from his father strict principles of loyalty and attachment to the crown, and being known to be a faithful adherent to the house of Stuart, he was considered a suitable person to be placed at the head of the Seventh Regiment of Cuirassiers, now Fifth Dragoon Guards, at the critical period when the proceedings of the court had alarmed the nation, and commotions were expected to follow; but he was soon afterwards relieved from that charge by an officer of more experience in military affairs, and appointed to the important trust of Governor of Hull. This place he held in the interest of James II. at the Revolution in 1688; but he was surprised and made prisoner by Colonel Copeley, and a party of men who had taken arms and declared for the Prince of Orange. His lordship was not afterwards employed in any public capacity; and he died in 1703.

RICHARD HAMILTON,

Appointed 15th February, 1687.

RICHARD HAMILTON was many years in the service of Louis XIV. of France, during the period that monarch was permitted, by King Charles II., to employ an English regiment of horse and one English and one Scots brigade of foot in his service. While engaged in the French wars he acquired the character of a gallant and enterprising officer; and he quitted the service of Louis XIV. when Charles II. demanded the return of his subjects from France in 1678. On the breaking out of Monmouth's rebellion he raised a troop of dragoons for the service of King James II., and was afterwards appointed colonel of one of the regiments of dragoons embodied at that period. After the suppression of the rebellion he was sent with his regiment to Ireland, and being a Papist and an officer of experience, he assisted Tyrconnel in remodelling the Irish army, by

dismissing the Protestants and replacing them with Papists. His fame as an officer, and his zeal for his religion, occasioned him to be placed at the head of the Seventh Regiment of Cuirassiers; but the remodelling of the English army was not completed when the Revolution took place, and the Roman Catholic officers and soldiers were placed in confinement. At this period Earl Tyrconnel had given out new commissions for levying thirty thousand men in Ireland, and reports were spread that a general massacre of the Protestants would take place; Richard Hamilton, though a Papist, was believed to be a man of honour, and he was known to have great influence with Tyrconnel, and also with the Irish Papists of all ranks, and having promised either to induce the Lord Lieutenant to resign the government, or to return and give an account of the negotiation, he was released from confinement and sent to Ireland; but on his arrival at Dublin he violated his engagement, and persuaded Tyrconnel to hold Ireland in the interest of King James. This breach of trust was rewarded with the rank of lieutenant-general, and an important post in the Irish army; but he did not long enjoy his new honours,—having been wounded and taken prisoner at the battle of the Boyne. Immediately after he was made prisoner, he was brought into the presence of King William, who put some questions to him respecting the Irish army, which he answered in the affirmative, and added the words *upon my honour*: the King repeated the words *your honour!* and turned from him, which was all the rebuke His Majesty gave him for his faithless conduct. He remained a prisoner until the termination of the war in Ireland, when he was exchanged for Lord Mountjoy, and proceeding to France, he appears to have passed the remainder of his life in that country.

JOHN COY,

Appointed 31st December, 1688.

This officer served a short time with the French army in the reign of Louis XIV., and afterwards commanded a troop in the Duke of Monmouth's regiment of horse, which regiment was disbanded in 1678. In 1680 he raised a troop of horse for service at Tangier in Africa; this

fortress being besieged by the forces of the Emperor of Morocco, he proceeded to that country immediately, and distinguished himself in action with the Moors. In 1683 his troop of horse was constituted Royal Dragoons; with which corps he continued to serve, and was engaged at the battle of Sedgemoor in 1685. In 1686 he was appointed Lieutenant-Colonel of Shrewsbury's Cuirassiers: and at the Revolution in 1688 he was promoted to the Colonelcy of the regiment; with which he served with distinction in Ireland and Flanders. Having become infirm from age and long service, he obtained the King's permission to dispose of his commission, in 1697, to the Earl of Arran; and from this period he led a retired life until his decease.

CHARLES EARL OF ARRAN,

Appointed 1st July, 1697.

This nobleman descended from the illustrious family of Butler, so renowned in the past ages for the many valiant, and loyal persons it has produced. He was the second son of Thomas Butler Earl of Ossory, (a nobleman distinguished for deeds of valour, loyalty to his sovereign, and the mild and social virtues which rendered him an ornament to society,) and grandson of the celebrated James, *first* Duke of Ormond. Having served under King William III. in Ireland and Flanders, where he evinced the same martial spirit and private virtues which had adorned his ancestors, he was elevated to the peerage of Ireland in January, 1693, by the titles of Baron of Cloghgrenan in the Queen's county, Viscount of Tullo in the county of Cutherlough, and EARL OF the islands of ARRAN in the county of Galway; he was also, at the same time, created an English peer by the title of Lord Butler, of Weston, in the county of Huntingdon. On the 16th of February, 1694, he was promoted to the colonelcy of a newly raised regiment of horse (which was disbanded at the peace of Ryswick), and in the summer of 1697 he purchased the colonelcy of the SIXTH HORSE, now Fifth Dragoon Guards. In March, 1703, he was promoted to the colonelcy of the Third Troop of Life Guards, which gave him the privilege of taking the court duty of gold stick in waiting to

Queen Anne; in 1712 Her Majesty constituted him Master-General of the Ordnance in Ireland; and in the following year appointed him Governor of Dover Castle, and Deputy Warden of the Cinque Ports. Soon after the accession of King George I. his Lordship was elected Chancellor of the University of Oxford. After the impeachment of his brother, James, second Duke of Ormond, for high treason, the Earl of Arran quitted the army. In February, 1716, he was constituted Lord High Steward of Westminster: and in 1721 he was permitted, by an Act of Parliament, to purchase his brother's forfeited estates. He died on the 17th of December, 1758, at the advanced age of eighty-eight years.

WILLIAM CADOGAN,

Appointed 2d March, 1703.

WILLIAM CADOGAN descended from a family of great honour and antiquity in Wales; and having embraced the profession of arms, he distinguished himself under King William III. in Ireland and Flanders, and was appointed major of the Inniskilling Dragoons. On the breaking out of hostilities in 1701, his great merit and abilities, which had become conspicuous in the preceding war, occasioned him to be promoted to the rank of colonel in the army, and appointed (1st June, 1701) quartermaster-general of the troops sent to Holland. He eminently distinguished himself under the great Duke of Marlborough, whose confidence and esteem he possessed in a high degree, and was promoted, in 1703, from the Inniskilling Dragoons to the colonelcy of the SIXTH HORSE. Advancing with the army into Germany he signalized himself at the battle of Schellenberg, on the 2d of July, 1704, where he had several shots through his clothes, and was wounded in the thigh. At the battle of Blenheim he evinced that undaunted bravery and greatness of soul with which he was signally endowed, and was promoted immediately afterwards to the rank of brigadier-general. In the following year he again signalized himself at the forcing of the French lines, where his regiment defeated the Bavarian Guards and took four standards; and in the memorable battle of Ramilies, fought on the 23d of May, 1706, he acquired new honour, and was

despatched shortly after the action with a body of troops to summon Antwerp, which fortress surrendered to him in a few days. On the 16th of August he commanded a body of troops employed in covering a foraging party near Tournay, and advancing with his characteristic boldness too near the town, he was surprised by a party of the enemy and made prisoner; he was, however, released on his parole three days afterwards, and was subsequently exchanged for Baron Palavicini. In January, 1707, he was promoted to the rank of major-general, and he was afterwards appointed minister plenipotentiary to the government of the Spanish Netherlands, in which employment he evinced the most admirable dexterity in business, and a peculiar aptitude in conducting negotiations. He commanded the van of the army in the movements which preceded and led to the battle of Oudenarde in 1708, and on this occasion his peculiar merits again shone forth; also in the part which he took in covering the siege of Lisle, in the action at Wynendale, and in forcing the passage of the Scheldt; and on the 1st of January, 1709, he was promoted to the rank of lieutenant-general. On the day preceding the battle of Malplaquet he was sent to confer with the French commander, and when near the enemy's position he indicated to a colonel of artillery, by dropping his glove, the spot where a battery was to be placed on the following morning, which proved of great importance. During the siege of Mons he went voluntarily into the trenches to encourage the soldiers in the attack of a ravelin, when his aide-de-camp was killed at his side, and he was dangerously wounded in the neck. Every additional campaign added new lustre to his rising reputation, and in that sublime display of military talent by which the French lines were forced in the summer of 1711, and Bouchain captured, he performed a distinguished part, as detailed in the Historical Record of the Fifth Dragoon Guards. When political events occasioned the removal of the Duke of Marlborough from all his appointments dependent on the crown, Lieutenant-General Cadogan, who had shared with this illustrious commander in his toils, dangers, and triumphs, and who, like him, was stedfast in his devotion to

the Protestant interest, and to the succession of the house of Hanover, was removed from his appointments of quartermaster-general and governor of the Tower, and called upon to dispose of his regiment for three thousand pounds to General Kellum. He was soon afterwards gratified by witnessing the accession of King George I., by whom he was appointed Colonel of the Second Foot Guards, Master of the Robes, and envoy extraordinary and plenipotentiary to the States General of Holland, in which capacity he conducted negotiations of great importance, and displayed those gifts of nature with which his mind was adorned; and while thus employed he was appointed Governor of the Isle of Wight. On the breaking out of the rebellion of the Earl of Mar, he changed the labours of the cabinet for those of the field, and in the depth of winter, in the midst of the most piercing frosts and snow, he evinced unshaken perseverance in extinguishing the flame of rebellion in Scotland, and was made a Knight of the most ancient order of the Thistle. On the 30th of June, 1716, he was elevated to the peerage by the title of LORD CADOGAN, Baron of Reading. In the autumn of the same year he was again sent as plenipotentiary to the States of Holland; on his return in 1717 he was sworn of the Privy Council, and afterwards promoted to the rank of general; and in May, 1718, he was created Baron of Oakley, Viscount of Caversham, and EARL CADOGAN. He was subsequently employed in negotiations of an important character with the house of Austria, Court of Spain, and States of Holland; and on the decease of the Duke of Marlborough in 1722, he was appointed General Commanding-in-Chief of the army. This distinguished nobleman died on the 17th of July, 1726, and was buried in Westminster Abbey.

GEORGE KELLUM,

Appointed 22d December, 1712.

GEORGE KELLUM obtained the commission of cornet in the Earl of Shrewsbury's regiment of horse, now Fifth Dragoon Guards, when that corps was embodied in 1685, and he served in Ireland and the Netherlands, under King William III. Having been promoted to the

lieutenant-colonelcy, he commanded the regiment in the wars of Queen Anne, and was promoted to the rank of colonel in the army in 1703. In the following year he distinguished himself at the battle of Schellenberg, and led the regiment to the charge with signal gallantry at the glorious battle of Blenheim. At the forcing of the French lines in 1705, he acquired additional laurels; and at the memorable battle of Ramilies, the squadrons under his orders were again victorious. In 1707 he was promoted to the rank of brigadier-general; in 1708 he commanded a brigade at the battle of Oudenarde; and in 1709 at that of Malplaquet; in 1710 he was promoted to the rank of major-general; and in 1712 to that of lieutenant-general; and in the same year he purchased the colonelcy of the regiment in which he had served so many years: he was, however, removed in 1717, and died on the 27th of December, 1732.

ROBERT NAPIER,

Appointed 27th May, 1717.

This officer was appointed cornet in the SIXTH HORSE, now FIFTH DRAGOON GUARDS, in January, 1692, and served with the regiment in the Netherlands until the peace of Ryswick. In 1702 he was promoted to the majority, and while serving with his regiment in Germany he was severely wounded at the battle of Schellenberg. In 1705 he was with his regiment at the forcing of the French lines, and in 1706 he was at Ramilies, and was promoted to the rank of colonel in the army a few days after the battle. He continued to serve at the theatre of war; was appointed brigadier-general in 1711; and obtained the colonelcy of the regiment in 1717. He was promoted to the rank of major-general in 1727; and to that of lieutenant-general in 1735: and died on the 10th of November, 1739.

CLEMENT NEVILLE,

Appointed 6th May, 1740.

CLEMENT NEVILLE entered the army at the Revolution; his first commission being dated the 6th of December, 1688, and after serving with distinction in the wars of King William and Queen Anne, he was promoted to the rank of colonel in the army at the close of the campaign

of 1711. On the 9th of April, 1720, King George I. conferred on him the colonelcy of the Fourteenth Dragoons, from which he was removed in 1737 to the Eighth Dragoons, and in 1739 he was promoted to the rank of major-general. The colonelcy of the SIXTH HORSE was conferred on this veteran in the following year; he was promoted to the rank of lieutenant-general in 1743; and he died in August, 1744.

RICHARD VISCOUNT COBHAM,
Appointed 5th August, 1744.

SIR RICHARD TEMPLE served under King William in the Netherlands, and on the breaking out of the war of the Spanish succession, he was promoted to the colonelcy of a newly-raised regiment of foot, which was disbanded at the peace of Utrecht. He served under the great Duke of Marlborough, and was conspicuous for a noble bearing, a greatness of soul, and a contempt of danger, which he exhibited in a signal manner at the sieges of Venloo and Ruremonde, at the battle of Oudenarde, and at the siege of the important fortress of Lisle. In January, 1709, he was promoted to the rank of major-general, and his conduct at the siege of Tournay, the sanguinary battle of Malplaquet, and siege of Mons, was rewarded, in the following year, with the rank of lieutenant-general and the colonelcy of the Fourth Dragoons. He served under the Duke of Marlborough in 1711, and had the honour of taking part in the forcing of the French lines at Arleux, and the capture of the strong fortress of Bouchain. After the change in the ministry and the adoption of a new system of policy by the court, the well-known attachment of this officer to the Protestant succession, occasioned him to be removed from his regiment; but on the accession of King George I. he was elevated to the peerage by the title of BARON OF COBHAM, and in 1715 he was appointed Colonel of the Royal Dragoons. In 1717 he was appointed Governor of Windsor Castle; in 1718 he was advanced to the dignity of VISCOUNT COBHAM; and in 1721 he was removed to the King's Horse, now First Dragoon Guards. He was also one of the Privy Council, and Governor of the island of Jersey; but resigned his appointments in 1733. On the change

of the ministry in 1742 he was promoted to the rank of field-marshal, and in December of the same year King George II. conferred upon him the colonelcy of the First troop of Horse Grenadier Guards. In 1744 he was removed to the SIXTH HORSE, and in 1745 to the Tenth Dragoons, the colonelcy of which corps he retained until his decease in 1749.

THOMAS WENTWORTH,

Appointed 20th June, 1745.

THOMAS WENTWORTH was appointed to a commission in the army on the 10th of March, 1704, and served several campaigns in the wars of Queen Anne. In December, 1722, he was promoted to the rank of colonel in the army, and in 1732 he was appointed colonel of the Thirty-ninth Foot, from which he was removed in June, 1737, to the Twenty-fourth Foot. Two years afterwards he was appointed brigadier-general; in 1741 he was promoted to the rank of major-general; and in 1745 he was appointed to the colonelcy of the SIXTH HORSE, which corps became the SECOND IRISH HORSE in the following year. He served the crown in a diplomatic as well as a military capacity, and died at the court of Turin in November, 1747.

THOMAS BLIGH,

Appointed 22d December, 1747.

This officer entered the army in the reign of King George I.; rose to the rank of Lieutenant-colonel of the SIXTH HORSE, and in December, 1740 he was appointed Colonel of the Twentieth Regiment of Foot. On the 27th of May, 1745, he was promoted to the rank of brigadier-general; was removed to the Twelfth Dragoons in the following year, and promoted to the rank of major-general in 1747. He was removed to the colonelcy of the SECOND IRISH HORSE in December of the same year; and was promoted to the rank of lieutenant-general in 1754.

War having commenced between Great Britain and France in 1756, Lieutenant-General Bligh was appointed, in the summer of 1758, to the command of an expedition designed to make a descent on the coast of France, with the view of causing a diversion in favour of the army

commanded by Prince Ferdinand of Brunswick in Germany. The fleet sailed in the beginning of August, and in seven days arrived in Cherbourg roads. The troops were landed, the town of Cherbourg was captured, the harbour, pier, and forts were destroyed, and the brass ordnance brought away as trophies of this success. In September a landing was effected on the coast of Brittany with the view of besieging St. Maloes; but this being found impracticable, the troops, after marching a short distance up the country, retired and re-embarked at the bay of St. Cas. The enemy advanced in great numbers under the command of the Duke of Aguillon, and attacking the rear of the British army, occasioned great loss. Lieutenant-General Bligh was much censured for his conduct on this occasion, and soon after the return of the expedition, he retired from the service.

HON. JOHN WALDEGRAVE,

Appointed 23d October, 1758.

The HON. JOHN WALDEGRAVE obtained a commission in the First Foot Guards in 1737; in July 1743, he was appointed captain-lieutenant in the Third Foot Guards; in September following he obtained the command of a company, and in 1748 he was promoted to the commission of major in the same corps. On the 26th of June 1751, he was promoted to the colonelcy of the Ninth Foot; he was removed to the Eighth Dragoons in 1755; and to the SECOND IRISH HORSE in 1758. Having been promoted to the rank of major-general, he proceeded to Germany, and commanded the brigade of infantry which so highly distinguished itself in 1759, at the battle of Minden, where his gallantry and extraordinary presence of mind at a critical moment decided the fate of the day. In September of the same year he was removed to the Second Dragoon Guards, and continuing to serve in Germany during the remainder of the seven years' war, gave signal proofs of ability and valour in numerous actions with the enemy, and was equally conspicuous for kindness of heart and regard for the soldiers who served under his orders. In 1763, he succeeded to the title of EARL WALDEGRAVE; he was afterwards advanced to the rank of general,

and in 1773, he obtained the colonelcy of the Second Foot Guards, which he retained until his decease in October 1784.

HON. JOHN FITZ-WILLIAM,

Appointed 27th November 1760.

The HON. JOHN FITZ-WILLIAM obtained a commission of captain and lieutenant-colonel in the First Foot Guards, in 1745; was promoted to the colonelcy of the Second or Queen's Royal Regiment of Foot in 1755; and in June, 1759, he obtained the rank of major-general in the army. In the following year he was removed to the colonelcy of the SECOND IRISH HORSE; was promoted to the rank of lieutenant-general in 1761; to that of general in 1783; and died in 1789.

JOHN DOUGLAS,

Appointed 27th August, 1789.

JOHN DOUGLAS was many years an officer in the Second Dragoons (Scots Greys), with which corps he served at the battle of Fontenoy in 1745. He was promoted to the rank of captain in 1755; proceeded with the regiment to Germany in 1758, and was appointed major in the following spring. He served four campaigns under Prince Ferdinand of Brunswick in Germany, and was at numerous battles and skirmishes. In 1770, he was promoted to the lieutenant-colonelcy of the Scots Greys; he was advanced to the rank of colonel in the army in 1775, and to that of major-general in February 1779. In April of the same year he was appointed Colonel of the Twenty-first Light Dragoons,—then first embodied and formed of the light troops belonging to certain dragoon regiments. At the termination of the American war in 1783, his regiment was disbanded; and in April 1787, he was appointed Colonel of the Fourteenth Foot: he was also promoted to the rank of lieutenant-general in the same year. In 1789, he was appointed to the colonelcy of the FIFTH DRAGOON GUARDS, which he retained until his decease, on the 10th of November 1790.

THOMAS BLAND,

Appointed 18th November, 1790.

This officer obtained a cornetcy in the Seventh Dragoons on the 30th of March, 1754, and continued in that regiment upwards of thirty-six years. He served three campaigns in Germany under the Duke of Brunswick; was appointed major of the regiment in 1765, and lieutenant-colonel in 1771. In 1782, he was promoted to the rank of major-general, and in 1790 he was appointed from the lieutenant-colonelcy of the Seventh Dragoons to the colonelcy of the FIFTH DRAGOON GUARDS. In 1796, he was promoted to the rank of lieutenant-general, and to that of general in 1781. He died on the 14th of October, 1816.

PRINCE LEOPOLD OF SAXE-COBURG,

Appointed 18th October, 1816.

This illustrious Prince, whose military services have become connected with the RECORD of the FIFTH DRAGOON GUARDS, by his appointment to the colonelcy of the regiment, entered the army of the Emperor Alexander of Russia in 1803, and rose to the rank of major-general; but in 1810, Bonaparte demanded that His Royal Highness should quit the Russian service, and the Prince was induced to acquiesce, in order to conciliate Napoleon, and to preserve the possessions of the house of Coburg from being seized on by the French. Prince Leopold was subsequently employed in negotiating an arrangement respecting the principality of Coburg, with the crown of Bavaria, in which he displayed superior diplomatic talents. At the commencement of 1813, he exerted himself, as far as his situation permitted, at that critical and momentous period, to prepare the emancipation of Germany, and in February he proceeded to Poland, to the Emperor of Russia, by whom he was cordially received, and a command in the Russian army was given to His Royal Highness. He was at the battle of Lutzen on the 2d of May; was subsequently sent by forced marches towards the Elbe, to support the Prussian General Kleist; but the Prince's destination was afterwards changed, and on the 19th of May he marched to support General Barclay de Tolly: His Royal Highness was, however, recalled, to take part in the battle of Bautzen, on the 20th and 21st of the same month; and after

supporting the line at various points, he covered the retreat on the evening of the second day, with the cavalry under his orders, amidst the hottest fire.

On the 26th of August His Royal Highness was detached to support the corps under Prince Eugene of Wirtemberg, posted near the fortress of Königstein; and Prince Leopold maintained, with his cavalry, a precarious position for five hours, against the repeated attacks of a force treble his own numbers, by which he defeated the designs of the enemy, and preserved Prince Eugene's troops from destruction. On the following day the corps took post beyond Pirna, which place the enemy took by storm, and endeavoured to extend with his cavalry upon the level ground near the Elbe; but was driven back by the troops under Prince Leopold. The main army, however, retired towards Bohemia, by which the retreat of the corps near Pirna was rendered difficult, and the abilities of His Royal Highness were particularly conspicuous in the masterly dispositions and skilful movements of the cavalry under his orders, in facilitating and covering the retrogade movement of the corps. A sharp action occurred in the village of Peterswalde on the 29th of August, when His Royal Highness signalized himself; several other actions occurred on the same day in the mountains, and towards the evening, the Prince repulsed the attack of a superior force near the village of Prisen, with signal bravery and astonishing success; and on the following morning he received from the Emperor Alexander the Cross of the military order of St. George. The action was renewed on the 30th of August, and the allied army having been concentrated, the French were defeated with considerable loss. Prince Leopold had a distinguished share in the engagement, and he pursued the retiring enemy to the village of Peterswalde: the brilliant conduct of His Royal Highness between the 26th and 30th of August, was rewarded by the Emperor of Austria with the military order of Maria Theresa.

Prince Leopold had a distinguished post at the battle of Leipzig, and, with the cavalry under his orders, contributed materially to the decisive

termination of that gigantic contest. His Royal Highness was actively employed in the beginning of 1814; was at the battle of Brienne, and in the pursuit of the defeated army on the 2d of February, and in several minor affairs. On the 25th of March the Prince was in the action with the French at La Fere Champenoise, when, attacking the enemy's right flank at Caunentrai, he carried the position, captured five pieces of cannon, and, when attacked in turn, he repulsed the enemy, and maintained his ground with signal intrepidity. The battle of Paris concluded the campaign, and on the 31st of March, the Prince entered that city with the cavalry of the reserve, and remained there in garrison. These important events were succeeded by the abdication of Napoleon, and, when the Congress assembled at Vienna, Prince Leopold of Saxe-Coburg conducted the business relating to his own country.

On the return of Bonaparte to France, in 1815, Prince Leopold proceeded to the grand army on the Rhine, and soon afterwards reached Paris. On the termination of the war he visited England; became a suitor to Her Royal Highness the Princess Charlotte of Wales, and, having obtained the consent of the Prince Regent, the nuptials between Prince Leopold of Saxe-Coburg, and the presumptive heiress to the British throne, were eventually solemnized.

On the 2d of May, 1816, Prince Leopold obtained the rank of general in the British service, and on the 24th of the same month he was promoted to the rank of field-marshal. The colonelcy of the FIFTH, OR PRINCESS CHARLOTTE OF WALES' REGIMENT OF DRAGOON GUARDS was conferred upon Prince Leopold in October of the same year, and he presented to the officers' mess a handsome service of plate. His Royal Highness was also honoured with the Order of the Garter, and the Order of the Bath; but in the midst of these accumulated distinctions he sustained the loss of his amiable consort, whose decease on the 6th November, 1817, occasioned the most sincere grief throughout the kingdom, and Prince Leopold was for some time inconsolable.

The events which transpired in the Netherlands in 1830, having led to the separation of several provinces from Holland, and to the formation of an independent state, called Belgium, Prince Leopold was invited to accept of the sovereignty of that kingdom in 1831, and His Royal Highness acquiesced. Thus the FIFTH DRAGOON GUARDS had the gratification of witnessing the elevation of their colonel to a throne.

On resigning the colonelcy His Royal Highness was pleased to cause the following farewell address to be sent to the regiment:—

"Claremont, 14th July, 1831.

"The Prince Leopold is desirous on quitting England, to communicate to his regiment, that the circumstances which call him to another country have made it necessary for him to relinquish the command of the corps; and he has reserved it, as one of his last and most painful duties, to bid them farewell. It would have been His Royal Highness's wish on this occasion, to have expressed personally to the regiment his regret in leaving them, and the sincere wishes he shall always entertain for their happiness and welfare; but their distant quarter, and the hurry which unavoidably attends his departure, render such a desire impracticable.

"In taking leave of the regiment, which it has been his happiness for so many years to command, many subjects press on His Royal Highness's attention that he would be anxious publicly to advert to; some of these bear paramount claim to his thankfulness and recollection; and it is such that he is chiefly solicitous to notice and record, on this last occasion of his addressing them:—he alludes particularly to the uniform maintenance of discipline, efficiency, and high character, which have marked the corps as one of the most distinguished in the service, throughout the long period he has known them;—this has been conspicuous, whether considered with respect to their efficiency in equipment,—their discipline and conduct in quarters,—or their movements and perfection in the field,—in every point, these have been eminently and invariably supported, and have established a name to the regiment, that, as it should be the first ambition, so it is among the highest rewards, a soldier can

know. To Lieutenant-Colonel Wallace, whose zeal and knowledge of the service have guided and perfected this state of discipline;—to the officers, who have ably and successfully devoted their efforts to uphold it;—to the non-commissioned officers and privates, who have maintained the discipline marked out to them, and, sharing the feelings of their officers in the character of the regiment, have by their conduct assisted to uphold it;—to one and all,—individually and collectively,—His Royal Highness returns his most hearty thanks, with his unqualified approbation of their conduct, under every view of discipline or exigency of service:—to such officers and to such men, it is unnecessary to say anything that can urge or stimulate their future zeal; His Royal Highness feels assured, that their Sovereign's approbation will ever remain their first aim, while *the name of the regiment*, deeply honoured by them and cherished in their hearts, will never cease to influence them in attaining that high distinction. His Royal Highness has always felt pride in being one of their number, and he can never cease to feel the truest interest in whatever can affect their name as a corps, or their welfare and happiness as individuals; and with his heartfelt wishes for the uninterrupted prosperity and perfection of both, he reluctantly bids them, Farewell.

(Signed) "ROBERT GARDINER.

"To Lieutenant-Colonel Wallace,
"Commanding Fifth Dragoon Guards."

SIR JOHN SLADE, BART., G. C. H.

Appointed 20th July, 1831.

THE END.

Printed in Great Britain
by Amazon

25157431R00061